My Summer of '69

Penelope Gardiner

My Summer of '69

Contents

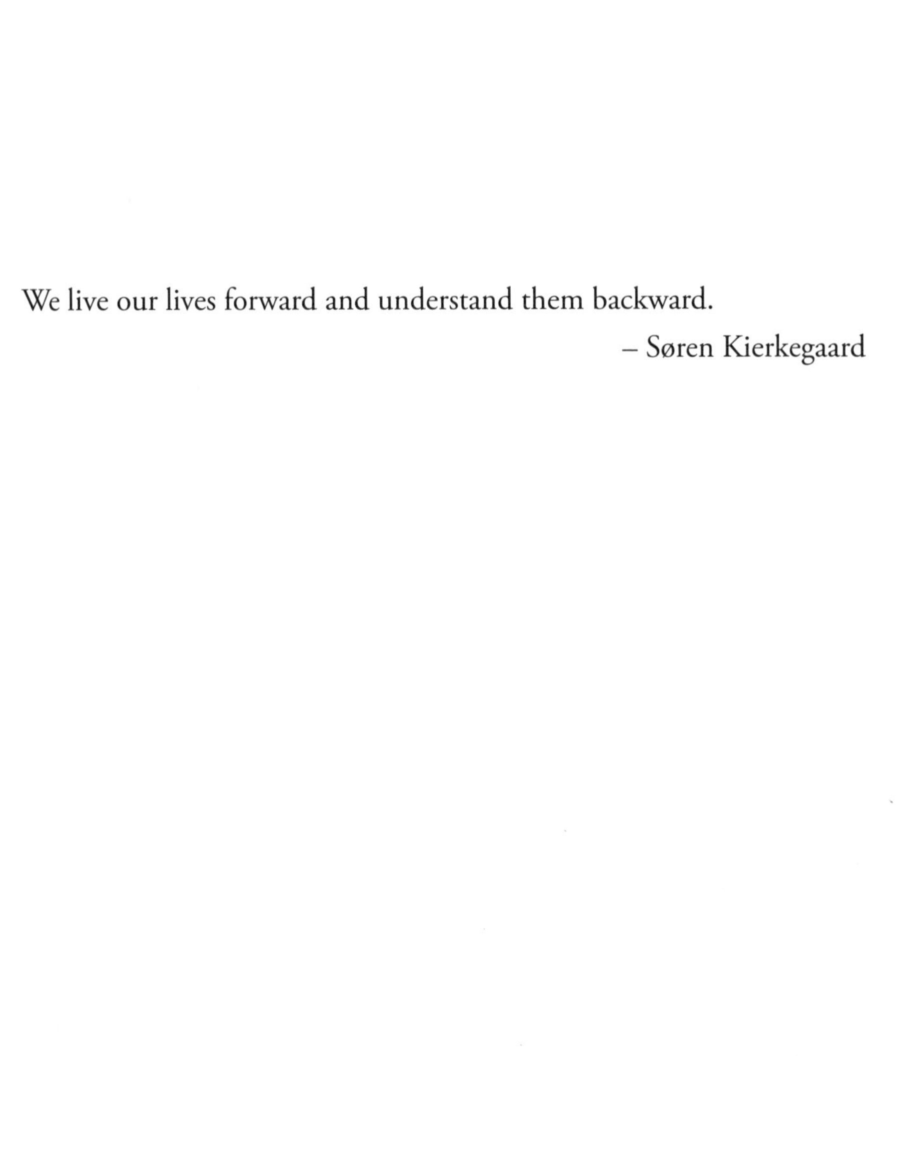

We live our lives forward and understand them backward.

– Søren Kierkegaard

1. I Meet the Man in Black

I first became aware of the infamous Tom Corley as 'the man in black' who used to come down to the beach every afternoon. Tom was an enigma, a rather solitary figure, who at 33 years of age did not welcome any intrusion into his privacy. I was a 22-year-old virgin from New Zealand with no real-world experience. But I was open to everything new the world could throw at me.

I didn't know anything about him when I first laid eyes on him, tall and slim, black jeans, black shirt, black boots, and black sunglasses, anxiously scanning the beach looking for his staff whom he had fired the night before (this apparently occurred on a regular basis). The staff were strangely only too happy to go back with him to the Dubliner Bar, for another night of madness and mayhem, usually ending up with the punters all being thrown out at 3 o'clock in the morning, including the staff. When I say 'infamous', not a lot was known about him, as he had created an air of mystery around himself, but in such a small village, it was impossible to not know who he was.

In those days, meaning the 60s in Franco's Spain, Sitges was a small enclave on the Mediterranean coast, an hour south of Barcelona on the train, or 40 minutes on the terrifying coastal road, consisting of hairpin bends and huge coastal drop-offs, known to the locals as the 'Road of Death'. Sitges had remained untouched by all the huge developments taking place further down the coast in Torremolinos and Marbella, but it was fast becoming *the* place to go on your 'tour de España', for reasons I was about to find out.

To be truthful, I was enthralled by the place from day one, a picture-postcard Spanish town with golden sand beaches, and in those days, the fishermen's boats drawn up on the shore as they unloaded their shining baskets of sardines and prawns. Just above the beach was the Paseo Maritimo (seafront promenade) where all the best, and most expensive restaurants were to be found. The town of Sitges stretched from there up to the plaza de la villa (village square) in the middle of town, and then downtown to all the tourist bars and cafes. I couldn't help it, I just fell in love with the place.

I had never been to the Dubliner, the Irish bar that Tom owned and ran in Calle Isla de Cuba (Cuba street) just off the town square and was in no hurry to do so, as I had heard of awful fights in there, including stories of guns lying about on the bar and blood running down the stairs. This sounds far-fetched I know, but there were mercenaries in town, recently out of the Belgian Congo, and the Dubliner Bar was where they all hung out.

In summer, just like all the tourist bars in the town, the Dubliner Bar was packed every night, mainly with Irish, Scottish, English, Australians, and Kiwis, all the big drinkers you could wish for. The bar itself, rather like its owner, was secretively tucked away on a residential street, up a flight of stairs with a small terrace outside overlooking the street; as opposed to all the bars in the Calle Dos de Mayo which was the big party venue downtown where all the tourists went, so you had to know about the Dubliner to find it and go there. I would eventually get to know it very well.

It was the 'summer of 69' in Spain and we partied hard every day. I had been hitch-hiking all over Europe, and had ended up in Sitges. It was known as a cool little village where a lot of the boys who had fought in Vietnam passed through on their way to Marrakesh. They had finished their 'tour of duty', signed off in Stuttgart, and made a beeline for Morocco, where they had heard the hash was plentiful and good.

I had only been living there for a few weeks, and was hanging with some young Americans who had, on this particular day my story begins, organised a boat to go out on the water for a few hours. Pay 100 pesetas and you had all the booze you could drink, guys with guitars, some sandwiches: one big bloody piss-up. A 100 pesetas in 1969 was about US$12.

It was a beautiful day, with some people smoking dope, (I think that was the whole idea of the boat trip as they couldn't be arrested by the Guardia Civil out at sea) and all of us just enjoying the sun and the crystal clear water. There were about 50 of us on board – foreigners from all over the world; pissed and stoned young people on an old, renovated fishing boat, that had been given a second chance.

After a beautiful, long hot day of cruising around the coast, swimming off the boat, and getting sunburned and slightly tipsy, we finally arrived back at the port and a few of us found our way to Duncan's Bar. This was a little bar at the bottom of town, near the waterfront, where the smell of the salty sea breeze and the delicious aroma of sardines being grilled down on the beach hung in the air, along with the homey smell of Coppertone suntan lotion. This bar was owned by a Canadian guy, Duncan, where I had a spot singing with a band from Birmingham and where I sang for my drinks every night. I don't remember how I got that job, but I loved it, singing my favourite songs by the Dubliners, a very famous Irish folk group at the time.

There were four of them in the band, lovely guys, whom I really didn't know very well, and we sang mostly Irish songs, 'Black Velvet Band' and 'I'm a Rover' being great favourites. Unbeknownst to me, Duncan was one of Tom's best friends, so Tom was in the bar that night.

Apparently, although I never saw him, he saw me singing and went back to the Dubliner Bar and sent his sidekick Tony to approach me. We all knew Tony was Tom's 'go to' man, who would do his bidding, no matter what the task. Tony was English and was known by several monikers, including Dirty Tony, Tony Fix It and Tarragona Tony, for various, self-explanatory reasons. It was this 'person of many names' who approached me and said Tom wanted me to go up to the Dubliner. I flat out refused, saying I would never go to 'that place'. Then he said, "Well, Tom would like to take you out to dinner."

Whoa! This was a whole different ball game. We didn't do *dinner* in those days. I had become addicted to the custard-filled donuts I had recently discovered in Spain, so that was usually my breakfast. For lunch I would join my American mates driving to the little pueblo of San Miguel de Orlèrdola up in the hills behind the town, where we had found a typical Spanish restaurant that served 'pan tostado con tomate y ajo' (grilled bread with tomato, garlic and olive oil), and maybe a lamb chop, if you were feeling rich. We spent many amazing days up there, drinking all day, sleeping it off in the church next door, and starting all over again. If you ordered a pan tostado for 25 pesetas (US$3) you got a free bottle of red wine.

So, as I was not in the habit of eating dinner, (or, more correctly, couldn't afford to) this was a very tempting offer, and also, I was intrigued by the man in black that I had seen on the beach. So, abandoning all caution, and to start off the beginning of the rest of my life, I went with Tony up to the Dubliner.

I shall never forget walking up the steps and into the bar for the first time and catching Tom's eye. I have no idea what I was wearing; it would have been a version of jeans and a T-shirt, and bare feet, but I remember the exact moment as if it were yesterday. Tom walking down the length of the bar and coming over to me and walking me back down the stairs, and it sounds completely crazy, but that night I knew something special was happening. I had heard of 'love at first sight' and now I really felt this could be it.

From day one, it was all just terribly exciting. He was a very charismatic man, and I was totally entranced. He asked me where I would like to go to dinner, and I knew exactly where I wanted to go, as I had always imagined having dinner there. So, we made our way to the beautiful little restaurant I had in mind, with tables outside on the narrow footpath, with hanging baskets of flowers, and Spanish guitar music playing softly inside. I walked past this restaurant every day on my way to the beach, and I had always dreamed of having a meal there one day. I can no longer remember the name of this little Spanish restaurant, but it looked so beautiful and authentic, on one of the myriad streets of steps leading down to the water.

I don't remember what we had to eat or what we talked about, but I was sure I was in love by the end of the night.

Since I had arrived in Sitges a couple of months before, I had found a place to stay with three American guys, Russ, Pete, and Cowboy John, who all had jobs in different bars in town. They generally slept all day and worked and partied all night, so I hardly ever saw them, although Tom thought they were losers and bums and wasn't very impressed that I lived with them. They thought I was very strange as I didn't smoke or do drugs which I have never done in my life, but they liked me as I looked after their puppy whose name was Dog. The only thing that stands out in my relationship with them was the day the town police knocked on the door looking for drugs, when Russ came bounding up the stairs with a small bag of hash insisting that I flush it down the loo in my bathroom. (Nice of the police to knock I remember thinking.)

As we were leaving the restaurant on that first dinner date, Tom had asked me out for lunch the next day and, although I knew I was very involved by now, I had already made plans to go on a road trip to the south of France and on to Sardinia with my girlfriend, Gayle, a ballet dancer from South Africa. I couldn't let her down at the last minute, so Tom gave me a letter for a friend of his in Sardinia asking him if he could give us a job in his nightclub. We were planning to hitch-hike up to the Spanish border and on to the south coast of France, before taking a ferry to Corsica, which would only take us a few days.

It felt very strange just leaving him like that after one date, but I couldn't let my friend down, and I had the feeling he would wait for me; well I was hoping. We only planned to be away for a few weeks, and

I knew it was Tom's busiest time of the year in the Dubliner, so although it was hard, I felt very positive about continuing with my plans.

Let's just say, as I had never been 'in love' before, I wasn't too sure what it felt like, but for the moment I was happy that it all felt terribly romantic – and it could wait.

2. My Earliest Memories

To go right back to the beginning, up until the moment I met Tom, I had led what could be described as a fairly normal life in New Zealand, with an absolutely idyllic childhood, living on a large sheep and cattle farm in the 'wop wops' of Manawahe, in the Bay of Plenty, with my mum and dad and five younger sisters. There were no shops, just the local school, gravel roads and of course, no TV.

I started Manawahe school in 1951 when I was still four years' old; probably because mum had had enough of me at home, as I was evidently a 'bit of a handful'. I caught the bus to school the first day and I was so excited as I couldn't wait to leave home. There is a photo of me in my little striped summer frock, holding my black cat, Nugget, whom I was hoping I could take with me to school.

I just couldn't wait to get to school, even though I had no idea what was in store for me there. On my first day all the kids lined up outside the schoolroom when the headmaster, Mr Noonan, rang the old cow bell, and then he played folk music on the gramophone, and we all marched around and did Scottish dancing; our PE for the day. This is the same Mr Noonan who later gave me the strap out in the school corridor when I was ten: man it hurt! I must have done something pretty bad to merit getting the strap, as usually only the boys got hit.

I was the only kid in Primer 1, and was made to sit up the front of the 25 kids of all ages sitting behind me, ranging from age four to 14. We were all taught by the one teacher, Mr Noonan, in the same building. These older kids basically stayed at primary school until they could legally leave at age 15, having no high school to go to in the immediate vicinity.

I mastered my Primer 1 book *Janet & John,* having learned to read fairly precipitously. I just loved learning to read so much; reading was almost like a drug to me.

As I grew older three other kids joined me in my class. We were basically given an arithmetic book for the first hour, an English grammar book for the second hour and a social studies book for the third hour, until 12 o'clock which was lunchtime. With so many kids of different ages in that one room with one teacher, not too much actual 'teaching' got done.

After lunch you could do art in the tiny art room next door, but as I was really hopeless at art, I tended to skive off whenever I could to go and play by myself. Our art teacher was Miss Price, a tiny freckled young thing who didn't really have a lot to do.

One afternoon when Mr Noonan had left in the bus to take the kids home who lived around 'the loop' (the opposite direction to where I lived), Miss Price set up a small gramophone and played me her Elvis Presley records. I thought I had died and gone to heaven, listening to Elvis belting it out in the wilds of Manawahe. My very first taste of rock and roll. I was 8 years' old.

Often in the summer, after lunch, we would all get on the bus, and some of the parents took kids in their cars, and we drove to Lake Rotoma, about half an hour away, for swimming lessons. The lake was surrounded by New Zealand native bush and we kids had found a big rata vine (a Tarzan-like vine) in the bush and used it to swing out over the lake, and when you fell in, you dog-paddled to shore – that was called 'swimming lessons'.

We had an awful lot of freedom at school, and I would play for hours on my own. We also played serious games of marbles with the boys, digging holes in the clay tennis court (no tennis was ever played), or built houses out of ti-tree, (or Manuka as it is known today) in the 'horse paddock'. On occasion I rode my horse to school, but as this took nearly two hours it wasn't a regular thing.

Back at home, our neighbours, the three Schick boys Bobby, David and Trevor, lived on the farm opposite ours and were our best friends, and we three oldest sisters, me, Robby and Judi, spent hours with these guys, climbing trees, making treehouses, and eeling in the Phillips' stream where we wriggled on our stomachs into a cave whose walls were covered with big wetas. (Google NZ Weta – they are scary monsters).

Bobby Schick built us a playhouse from the large box Mum's new piano had been packed in. Dad had bought a piano for her when Funny Story, one of our racehorses, won a race. Dad was a very hard-working farmer, but his first real love was horses, specifically thoroughbreds, and I remember from a very early age his passion for racehorses, many of which he bred on the farm.

I would spend hours on my own, fighting make believe wars, (Us v Germans) in the front paddock till dark. It was normal for kids to play at wars, and especially in those days as our dads had recently come home from the Second World War. Our dad had fought there, even though he rarely spoke of his experiences.

We were so happy making our own entertainment. I used to write plays for my two younger sisters, Robby and Judi, to perform in with me, dressing us all up in Mum's old clothes. I was also a voracious reader and Mum had joined me up to two book clubs. However, as well as the book clubs, I went through Mum and Dad's whole bookcase, reading everything from Readers Digest books to every book on horses known to man, plus *Forever Amber* and the entire Hornblower series, which was absolutely my favourite. But, most of all, I was out riding my horse.

Dad put me on a horse before I could walk, perched on a sheepskin on my first horse, Star. I only ever rode bareback as Dad didn't think it was necessary to give me a saddle, even though he had plenty of them in the stables. Then Dad gave us a beautiful palomino pony, Honey, so named after the beautiful honey-colour of her coat. She was a little devil and knew how to rub me up against the barbed-wire fence way up the hill, and then taking off for home, leaving me to follow after her on foot.

Dad had also caught and tamed a young filly, that he had found with a group of wild horses out the back of the farm. We named her Sugar, as she was of a much sweeter temperament than our moody, and often bad-tempered Honey, and was coloured a beautiful silvery grey.

I became friends with Helen in my class at school, who had a horse called Prince, and she would ride to our place in the weekends, or I would go to their farm in the Herepuru Road. These weekend rides, starting on a Saturday morning could take anything up to three hours on completely deserted country roads, on my own, but nobody ever worried about me or went looking for me. I must have been about 10 years' old at that stage. It was really peaceful and beautiful riding to their farm, and I never tried to hurry along, just enjoying the morning, with birdsong all around me and the sweet smell of the native bush.

On other weekends I rode my horse to stay with another friend Wynn, who lived over three hours in the opposite direction from our place. When our horses were worn out, we would build cardboard stables for our china horses, drawing and cutting-out and colouring saddles and bridles, and horse covers for them.

In the summer I used to creep out of my bedroom window at dawn and catch my horse to go for a ride before school. I was definitely a bit of a loner and didn't really have time to play with my other sisters.

One weekend Wynn rode her old horse Red all the way to our place in the very early morning. When she arrived we rode our horses straight to the top of Mount Misery, behind the Schick's house, and as we galloped back across the front paddock, poor old Red dropped dead of a heart attack! It was awful. Dad's friend Dave, who was also my godfather, was staying with us that weekend and Dad and Dave just happened to be all dressed up in their best suits ready to go to the Rotorua races. They had to get changed into their old clothes and gumboots and get out the shovels and dig a massive hole for Red where he lay.

When he wasn't working from dawn to dusk on the farm Dad could be found in the stable with his latest thoroughbreds, brushing them and talking to them. Dad, or Alan Thompson to you, had lost his right arm in the Second World War, and when I first went to school, all the kids teased me about my dad, calling him Captain Hook. I didn't know what they were talking about, so I had to go home and have a good look at my father to discover that yes, he had a hook on the end of his arm. I had never noticed it before; it was just Dad.

Dad's family were farmers near Whakatane, about an hour away from Manawahe, and he and his older brother, Rob had joined up when the fight against Hitler began. Rob had left New Zealand at the beginning of the war, and was killed in Libya, which Dad found out about on his way over in his ship. He also landed in North Africa, after which his battalion moved on to Italy, eventually making their way across the Apennines where Dad was badly injured in a tank accident and lost his right arm near Assisi. To say he was fairly pissed off about this would be a supreme understatement.

He eventually came back to New Zealand on a hospital ship and spent many months in various hospitals, recuperating and learning to do everything with his left hand. He was fitted with a prosthetic 'arm' which was strapped over his right shoulder and could be fitted with a hook, a scrubbing brush, a shovel holder and a weird-looking hand. And off he went to farm the land in Manawahe that his father had given him.

This was very hard land, and Dad needed a shepherd to work on the farm with him, so a new house was built in a paddock along the road from our house, for the shepherd and his family, who came up from Raetihi down country. As there were many other chores Dad couldn't attend to, such as fencing, another family was moved into the old house beside the woolshed, with Ted helping Dad in myriad ways.

Dad's nickname among his friends was 'Horse', as he was so

knowledgeable about horseflesh, and he eventually bred one of the most famous horses in New Zealand racing circles, Blue Blood.

How lucky he was to have met my beautiful mother, Pamela in 1946, who lived in the Bank of New Zealand in Whakatane. Her father was the Bank Manager, a 'very important person' in those days. Mum was a real town girl, who, after her marriage to Dad, was whisked up into the hills of Manawahe to become a farmer's wife. I think she had been a bit spoiled by my French grandmother, as she had never learned to cook and was flung into the role of cook to various shearing gangs and other workers on the farm. She did amazingly well, all things considered, but I never saw her venture outside the garden gate. She just simply wasn't interested in the doings on the farm.

However, she became a brilliant gardener, transforming the miserable overgrown lawn surrounding our old house into beautiful gardens over the years, which we all loved and were so proud of. We also had a grass tennis-court out the front of the house that Dad had made on the bulldozer, and as we grew older, many hotly-contested games of tennis were played there.

We didn't even try to beat Dad at tennis. He had played in a Bay of Plenty team before the war, and set about learning to play again with his left hand – he was very competitive that man. He taught me to play chess when I was about 10, and in all the games we played over the years, I could never beat him.

Our home was a tiny little farmhouse with three bedrooms, and one bathroom, and how she managed six daughters (well, I wouldn't say I was actually managed), shows her devotion to her husband and her girls. We were known as the best-behaved family in the Bay of Plenty!

Money was tight immediately after the war, and although we were of course well fed, with a sheep killed every week for the three families living on the farm, and produce from Dad's vegetable garden, we very quickly learned never to ask for anything. You were given a present on your birthday and at Christmas, otherwise, don't ask.

However, I remember I once did have the temerity to ask for a pair of jodhpurs that I had seen advertised in the Weekly News, and lucky for me, Mum wrote away to the firm in Christchurch and a beautiful new pair of jodhpurs eventually arrived for me. From then on I was very rarely seen to be wearing anything else – they were my absolute prized possession.

We were given tremendous freedom, with mum never knowing where we were from dawn to dusk in the school holidays, or even just after school. Horses were my life for many years, and I used to ride for miles and miles all over the farm, pretending I was in Wyoming (having of course read *My Friend Flicka* and *Green Grass of Wyoming*). I would stay out for hours on end until it was dark. I also built various jumps in the dog-kennel paddock and used to ride Honey bareback, doing circus tricks to show off to mum and dad and the sisters.

Mum and Dad usually drove to town (Whakatane) on a Friday afternoon, and I was left in charge of my younger sisters, a responsibility I affected to take seriously. However, I blotted my copybook one afternoon by persuading my three younger sisters to all climb onto the roof of the house with me. Mum and Dad arrived home early to see their whole family perched precariously up on the roof! There was hell to pay (for me).

Although we truly loved our life on the farm, we were lucky enough to spend our summer holidays at the surf beach of Ohope, over the hill from Whakatane. Before mum and dad built our beach house at Ohope, we used to stay in Uncle Jim's old army hut on the beach there. Jim was Dad's younger brother, who lived to a ripe old age, much loved by all his nieces. Those were glorious, long, hot summer days, eating cornflakes for breakfast out on the front steps in the sun, while Dad dug a new hole for the 'long-drop' (loo).

A friend of Mum and Dad's would sometimes take us to Ohiwa harbour, 20 minutes' away, to dig for cockles in the mud. These we boiled up in an old kerosene tin over a fire and which we ate with our fingers, soused in vinegar and wrapped in bread and butter right there on the beach.

By the time I went away to boarding school, Mum and Dad had bought their own property at Ohope, with a cute old bach on it, that we kids loved. But Mum had more lofty ideas about how she wanted her Ohope beach house to look, and designed and built a very modern, spacious 'party house' for her and Dad and all their friends, and ultimately, for me and my sisters and all our friends. People used to pull up in their cars driving past, as it looked as though our place was actually a very popular restaurant. Certainly some good times were had there over the years.

Christmas was always spent up at our maternal grandparents, the Kings' Takapuna house on the North Shore of Auckland city. (They had moved from Whakatane soon after Mum and Dad were married). We would drive up to Auckland, in those days about eight hours, with four little girls strung across the back seat of the car (no seatbelts) and were only allowed to stop once for a 'wee' at Paeroa, about half way into the trip. Many times (before the Auckland Harbour Bridge was built), we would arrive in Auckland City, only to find we had to join the end of a very long queue, all the way along Quay Street, waiting to get on the 'car ferry'. It was all very exciting, although probably not for Dad, who had already been driving for hours. We often didn't get on to the car ferry until after dark. We called the passenger ferries the 'sitting-down boats'.

I have wonderful memories of my maternal grandparents, who besides my mum, had two sons Ro and Perry, who were really more our friends than our uncles. Quite a lot of boozing went on in their house, all good stuff. Our poppa (the ex 'very important person') used to hide his small glasses of gin all over the house, and announce he was going for a lie-down, somewhere near to the hiding place of the drinks, known colloquially as 'spots'.

Driving to Biss & Thew Wine & Spirits in Poppa's Jag for the weekly booze supplies, we kids used to hide down on the floor of the car in embarrassment as Poppa swore at people's driving and shouted out the window at them. He was a real character, and normally a very mild-mannered man. This was a fellow who had won two Military Crosses on the Western Front in World War I. He was an absolute sweetheart, but my Gran was my favourite of them all. A wonderful cook, (she had a French father) who took the time that my mum didn't have, to teach me how to cook.

Gran had been the only child of her father's second marriage and was probably very spoilt. Rather unusually in those times she took to the stage, mainly acting in plays but also, in her younger days dancing in very elaborate costumes. She was a wonderful woman and I adored her. She met Poppa after the Great War and they married and lived happily together until his death. Gran then lived on in their big house in Takapuna with Uncle Roland.

Very suddenly, it seemed, those idyllic childhood years were over. Mum and Dad had decided I needed to go away to boarding school and they chose St Cuthbert's College 'for young ladies' in Auckland, where I started in 1960 at the ripe old age of 13. It was generally accepted in those days that kids on remote farms were sent away to school, and most of the boarding schools were 200 miles' away in Auckland. However, going from a carefree life and being left to myself for large periods of each day, to having to be completely conforming to a life where every move was monitored, did not suit me AT ALL. The only good part about it all was I met Lulu on my first day, and her fabulous mother, Hessey.

We were in a dorm together with three other girls and have remained good friends all our lives. Lulu and I were very similar in that we were both physically very immature, small and blonde and both loved horses. Lots of the girls were bigger and more mature than we were, so it meant we became inseparable.

Suffice to say I didn't enjoy my boarding school days and was even 'suspended' (no, not expelled) at one stage for going on a hunger strike. I figured if I went on long enough this could be my ticket home. However, being suspended for such a rebellious act only resulted in my being dragged in front of the headmistress and put on the bus home to face the wrath of my parents. After eight or nine long hours on the bus, I finally arrived at Lake Rotoma, where I could see Dad dressed in his suit (he always looked so handsome in his suit), sitting behind the wheel of our Pontiac. I had no idea what he had been told, but I thought he must be on his way to the Rotorua races, and I could get changed out of my uniform and go too.

This was not to be. Dad just loaded my suitcase in and turned the car around and drove me all the way back to Auckland (long day for me as it turned out). He gave me a great big lecture all the way, about how I had five younger sisters (as if I didn't know that) who all wanted to go to the same school (that I seriously doubted) and I had to start behaving myself, so to speak.

Just to explain about our unusual cars, in the years after the war it was very difficult to buy a decent car in New Zealand, and because farmers had overseas funds from exporting their beef, lamb and wool, their car dealers could order in cars from overseas not available to others. However, the catch was you more or less took the car on offer, which meant that one year we had a Pontiac, which all the Manawahe kids called the 'bag of bolts', and another year an Armstrong Sidley, which was an even more embarrassing car. We used to beg Dad to park way down the road away from the school when he needed to pick us up, so the other kids couldn't see our weird selection of cars.

While I was at boarding school, I would accompany Dad in the August holidays during lambing time. We would leave at 6 am on our horses, with five or six dogs for the day, and would take some sandwiches in our saddlebags, along with all the paraphernalia, injections, 'bearing' equipment, penicillin etc needed for the day.

We would ride way out the back of the farm, sometimes all day, lambing the ewes, and I dealt to a lot of 'bearing' ewes by myself and got used to helping ewes to have their lambs. (Maybe don't Google 'bearing ewes' - the illustrations may be a bit too explicit). I would go back to school with brown hands and face from being outside all day in all weathers.

Also in the winter, every Half Term, I was extremely lucky to be invited by Lulu's parents to go skiing at Mt Ruapehu in the centre of the North Island. They belonged to the Ruapehu Ski Club, where we all bunked down together and ate communal meals. I absolutely loved it, and Hessey lent me all the necessary ski gear. I would never otherwise have learned to ski without them.

In my final year at school, Lulu's parents took us to Surfer's Paradise in the May holidays. Lulu's dad Russ was another World War II soldier, who had been shot through the throat by the Germans and left for dead. Somehow, he lived through this and made his way back to New Zealand to marry the lovely Hessey.

It was my first time on a plane and my first time out of New Zealand, and I loved every minute of it. I took my surfboard with me, and Russ drove us up to Tweed Heads so I could surf Danger Point, along with all the Aussie boys. I didn't see any Aussie girls surfing and was given a bit of a hard time by these guys.

Anyway, as I thought, most intrepidly, I climbed down the cliff face with my board, flung it into the water (remembering that we didn't have a leg rope in those days) and caught a wave into the Tweed River. This lasted all of ten seconds when my board came to a shuddering halt, and I pitched over the front of it and into the water. I knew there were shark nets in the water and was hoping I was on the 'right' side of the net, which had caught the fin of my board. But a guy actually came over and helped me back on to my board and I gingerly paddled back in.

That same year, on the 23rd of November 1963, our headmistress gave us the terrible news that President Kennedy had been shot and killed in Dallas. There was no TV at our boarding school, so we were given the news in the school dining-room that night and we were all crying; my first real taste of world news impinging on my life – we all adored Jack Kennedy.

3. Freedom At Last

Finally escaping from St Cuthbert's boarding school at 17 years of age, I left, having passed my University Entrance exam, with absolutely no intention of going to university. The testimonial from the Head Mistress, Miss Violet Wood, was very succinct. Where my more well-behaved schoolmates had several pages attesting to their myriad achievements, mine read, "Hard-working, honest and enthusiastic".

After a year at the Auckland Technical Institute, I graduated as a shorthand typist and won a medal for 'Office Practice First in New Zealand – Penelope Thompson'. A shorthand typist was paid very good money back in the '60s, so Lulu and I had worked out that it would be the fastest way we could make money to leave 'this place', as I thought of New Zealand in those days.

Because of my extensive reading by this time, I was acutely aware of the fact that, from what I could see, people in other parts of the world had far more exciting and interesting lives than we did in New Zealand, and I was determined to redress the situation. It's just that we figured that New Zealand was at the bottom of the world, and we wanted to see the real thing in Europe, particularly Italy, Spain and Greece, but first of all, London.

While I was at the Technical institutre, as my parents couldn't yet conceive that I was growing up, (or maybe they did), they enrolled me in the Hostel of the Holy Name in Remuera in Auckland, known to everyone as 'The Nunnery'. There was a lot of escaping down the fire-escape and creeping back up again at night in that place, to the despair of the lovely nuns.

So, I was out of there after a year, only for my parents to insist that I get a job in our hometown of Whakatane, as private secretary to a friend of Dad's in a stock and station agency, I suppose, once again, to keep an eye on me. There I was sent to live with a dear old lady called Mrs Peck, who was also supposed to 'keep an eye on me'. Good luck with that, my dear lady. She rarely saw me – I really was free at last!

This is when I really took up surfing, as Ohope Beach was just over the hill from Whakatane, and there were plenty of good-looking young guys with cars and surfboard racks to drive me over there. I thought the guys who surfed were very cool and I wanted to be part of that culture. Also, at this stage I was so lucky to make friends with another girl from Whakatane, Shona, whom I had met coming and going on the train from school over the years. Shona was, and still is, a vibrant, beautiful blonde, always full of fun and still a great friend after all these years.

Shona was three years' older than me, and had a cute new Ford Anglia car, so she scooped me up and off we went on all kinds of surfing adventures. We were so lucky so have the beautiful Ohope beach on our doorstep, and I very quickly said adieu to Mrs Peck and moved into a seaside flat over there, with an Australian sheila, Brenda, where many wild beach parties were held.

Shona's car was named 'Calamity Jane', and many fabulous weekends were spent, loading our boards on to the roof rack, and hurtling off to wherever the surf was running. One winter's afternoon we were driving back from a weekend of surfing up the coast at Whangamata, and decided to drop in to see my cousin Scottie on his farm near Cambridge in the Waikato. I had introduced these two at my parents' holiday home at Ohope, as I loved them both and thought they would be perfect together. As it turned out, they were. They eventually got married and had three amazing kids.

I decided to make myself scarce so they could be alone together so I saddled Scottie's horse and went for a ride. It was quite late when I got back, and as they had imbibed quite a few gin and tonics during the afternoon, I was elected to drive home. I had had a few driving lessons with Dad in the driveway at Manawahe in my last year at school, but that was it for actually having driven a car, and I sure wasn't up to driving licence standards.

Off we went, bowling along in Calamity Jane, and halfway over the Mamaku hills, the car hit black ice, on which we spun around in circles until we flew over and over down a very steep cliff, coming to a stop on the car roof. Unbelievably, and despite the lack of seat belts, we seemed to be okay, albeit with lacy knickers from our baskets of clothes flying all around the car. I remember Shona had blood in her blonde hair, and I had a very sore chest from banging into the steering wheel, but, *amazingly*, no other injuries.

Somehow, we got out and climbed to the top of the cliff, and the first car to come along was driven by a young friend of ours, who said to me, "What the hell are you doing here, Chicken"? I was already not very popular with Shona's parents, and this definitely put me even more in their black books – they thought I was a bad influence. Who? Me?

Speaking of pre-seat belt times, it was also pre-wet suit times, when we used to surf in the winter. One freezing afternoon as we came in from a surf at Ohope, wearing no more than our usual bikinis and a jumper, we decided to stop off at the local dairy for a 'hot milkshake'. The dairy owner took one look at us, blue and shivering, and insisted we go into the back of the shop where she ran a hot bath for us.

Shona eventually left to go to London to meet up with Scottie, who had moved there the year before, so I took up with a friend John (Chook) Fowler, and with my girlfriend from school, Lulu. We too drove all over the North Island in his 'V-Dub bug' chasing the waves. In the winter we would often have a surf in the morning, then drive to the mountain and ski for the afternoon.

In between, we went to various race meetings around the North Island, and drove to hunt balls and parties down country. A hunt ball was held by myriad hunts where they chased hares not foxes, and were eagerly looked forward to as a 'hunting ground' for boys. You had to be invited by a partner and turn up in a long frock.

From 1964 to 1968 I was just generally enjoying life and saving money like mad, to leave this boring life behind. I hesitate to say I had lots of boyfriends, as it sounds a bit naff, but I did. However, they were all more friends than anything else, much as they may have tried to change that narrative. These were the very early sixties when there was no 'pill', and I had seen several of my boarding school friends having to go to stay in the South Island to have their baby, which was then adopted out. Unfortunately there was never any suggestion that the girls could keep their baby, as there was still a certain amount of shame involved in having a baby out of wedlock. This was the norm in the 1960s and was NOT going to happen to Miss Penelope Thompson.

And, to be fair, none of these boys really thrilled me to bits. I was having so much fun it just didn't matter. I was on track to saving enough money to get to Europe, and nothing could stop me. I had finally moved to Auckland to a very well-paying job during the day in the city, and was working nights as well in a small restaurant just down the road from my office.

Tony's was one of the first steak houses in Auckland city, and my two friends Trish and Marilyn worked there too. We wore red and white checked mini dresses and were hopeless waiters, but what fun we had! Marilyn is Marilyn Sainty, famous for her eponymous clothing shops in New Zealand, even today, and Trish Kilgour eventually married Geoff Chunn of Split Enz fame, and they also became well-known restauranteurs.

There were very few licensed restaurants in New Zealand in the 1960s (another good reason to get out of there I reasoned), and as Tony's wasn't licensed then, some of our clients would arrive with a nice bottle of French red, which we would decant into a teapot and serve in little teacups, as bottles on the table were against the liquor laws. What a godforsaken country!

So, in 1968 when we were both 20 years' old Lulu's wonderful mother, Hessey, who I had known and loved since our days in boarding school, had booked Lulu and I on the good ship *Orsova*, sailing to Europe. We had originally been booked on a ship to sail to Italy and had been enrolled at Perugia University for a year to learn Italian. That all sounded wonderful to me, but the Six Day War between Egypt and Israel, which had taken place in June 1967 meant that ship couldn't sail, as the Suez Canal had been shut and remained that way.

Hessey had found a P&O cruise named 'The New Way to Europe', which included ports in Sydney, Adelaide, Melbourne, Perth, Durban, and Capetown then across the Atlantic to Rio de Janeiro, and up the Brazilian coast to Salvador de Bahia, then back across the Atlantic to Casablanca and on to Lisbon and Southampton, taking six weeks in all.

So, in March 1968 we departed from Auckland, with all our friends and families there to see us off. We were so excited to finally be leaving New Zealand, and we didn't really think about when, if ever, we would be back. We were in a tiny cabin in the bowels of the ship, with an older English lady on her way back home to England, whom we called Mrs P. I'm sure she was quite happy to share the cabin with us as we were hardly ever there.

After calling in at the Australian ports, we crossed the Indian Ocean to Durban in South Africa, where we experienced our introduction to apartheid. We had booked a bus to drive across to Capetown with all our Aussie mates from the ship. However, as we were about to board the bus transfer, we (two small blonde females) were told we had to return immediately to the ship, as we didn't have a visa.

Apparently, because we were from New Zealand, we needed a visa to attest to the fact that we were less than 1/16th coloured. For some extraordinary reason the Aussies didn't need a visa. These were the awful apartheid years, and their rules meant that we therefore could not travel overland. This obviously came as a bit of a shock, even though we were very aware of the situation in South Africa back then.

So, we returned to the ship and sailed on to Capetown, where we disembarked and visited the beautiful wine country of Stellenbosch. Lulu and I got off the tour bus at the first vineyard we came to, and got so carried away sampling wines and talking to the locals, we missed getting back on the bus, to continue our tour. We whiled away the afternoon until the bus arrived to pick us up and take us back to the ship. Many years' later when I was visiting this fabulous region again with my sister, Anna, we actually passed by that same vineyard.

On board the ship we made some great friends at our dining-room table, including a couple of sisters from a sheep station in the Australian outback. However, our much more exciting friends were the Engineering Officers who lived below decks, where we spent most of our time partying. These guys were presumably working during the day (as engineers) but we only ever caught up with them at night and were invited down into their living quarters which were next to First Class and actually quite fancy. They were big party animals, and were always keen to go adventuring with us in nearly every port.

We finally sailed into Southampton, one day after my 21st birthday, rather hungover from the big party the lads put on for me the night before. From there we took the train up to London, thrilled to be in beautiful springtime England. But first, we had planned to go skiing in Lech in Austria, while we still had plenty of money. We stayed that night at the flat that Shona was renting in Palace Gardens Terrace in Kensington, behind the Russian Embassy, and left all our luggage there, including the enormous 'not wanted on voyage' suitcases, which had been stowed in the hold, and which we never opened again. Next day we boarded the train to Innsbruck at Victoria Station, so excited to be finally going to Europe to spend three weeks' skiing.

Lech was just a cute little ski village in those days, nothing like the resort of the rich and famous it has become today. We bought beautiful new skis, boots and ski gear, and spent fabulous long days catching the chairlift to Zurs and skiing all the way back, in time for 'sundowners' at the 'snow bar', drinking champagne laced with blood orange juice (or maybe that should be the other way round).

While there, I was sort of dating a chap called Ronald, one of the guys we met at our boarding house, the Madlockblick. Ronald was at Cambridge University back in England, and was a bit younger than me and very cute. He lived in Eaton Square in London. When we got back to London, he invited me up to Cambridge for the May Balls, and installed me in (and paid for) a bed and breakfast in the town, all very 'proper'.

I had bought four new ball dresses from Marks & Spencer, very inexpensively, one for each ball. I had a great time dancing into the night with all the young men there, and we also spent a fun day boating on the River Cam.

However, I wasn't that interested in poor old Ronald, who had also accumulated some black marks; notably by referring to us as 'colonials', and never inviting me to his flash house in Eaton Square, especially as he had come to our place for dinner several times.

Lulu and I had taken over Shona's flat when she left London to go back to New Zealand, and we both got really well-paying jobs in the West End, working as Private Secretaries, which sounds a little old-fashioned now, but that was what we were called. The office where I worked was in Marble Arch, which meant I could walk to work through Hyde Park every morning then back at night along Bayswater Road, visiting all our favourite pubs on the way home.

I worked for a Canadian mining company and my boss was a Colonel Boehm, a dear old fellow with a bristling moustache and a booming voice. He lived in a house called 1149, built in that year, in Aylesbury, Buckinghamshire, and was a heinous snob, but in a nice kind of way. When I asked him for the day off to go to the Queen's Garden Party, he looked genuinely shocked. What was this little New Zealand nobody doing attending the same garden party as he was invited to?

Colonel Boehm prided himself on belonging to the Royal Toxophilite Society, one of the oldest archery societies in Great Britain. Membership was through invitation only, with the Queen as their patron. I guess he thought of her and her garden party as his 'territory'.

On Friday nights Lulu and I would pour ourselves a glass of wine in our flat after work, get out our map of England and spread it on the floor, close our eyes and stick a pin into the map. Inevitably, no matter how far away it was, we would get on the train in the morning and travel to the chosen spot for the weekend. We proceeded to roam all over England, Wales and Scotland, staying in cute little bed and breakfast places most weekends. In one we had asked for the bathroom, which we were shown to, but found the bath full of coal!

The few weekends we didn't hop on a train to some part of the country, I managed to secure for myself a few plum babysitting jobs. We lived in a very upmarket area, with several embassies as our neighbours, including the Russian embassy, outside of which we witnessed some interesting demonstrations and 'sit-downs' led by the well-known pacifist, Bertrand Russell.

My favourite babysitting client was a Swedish Countess, who lived in a very beautiful town house not far from Ronald's house in Eaton Square. I was fascinated by the luxurious surroundings, and with the divine clothes the Countess wore – these babysitting jobs certainly opened my eyes as to how the 'other half' lived.

I became very friendly with Countess von Douglas, and she eventually offered me the fabulous job of looking after her 15 year old son in Kitzbühel when I was on my way to Germany later on in the piece.

From New Zealand Hessey had joined us up to an association called the Victoria League, where we were invited to soirées in elegant town houses in London, and where we met Princess Margaret who was the Patron. Through the Victoria League we were invited to the very swanky country homes of some very swanky people. I have no idea why they wanted to take in these scruffy little colonials, but they were invariably kind and not at all condescending, and we had some very enjoyable weekends out in the country.

We had some terrific adventures all through our year in London, and met so many lovely people, and I especially loved Ireland and its people, when we visited on our summer holiday. We had two weeks' summer leave, and had decided to take a gypsy caravan around the Ring of Kerry, and we started off with a 'hiss and a roar' with our horse, Charlie steadfastly sticking to his plodding pace of five miles a day. We were going nowhere, fast. When Charlie had completed his five miles he simply lay down in the road. We definitely needed to move a little faster than this if we were to complete our journey.

We met some guys from Newcastle in a quaint old Irish pub called Malone's, who had a green MG convertible, and from then on, we left Charlie to do his thing, and cruised around with the lads, after which we would find Charlie, and sleep in the caravan at night. Someone in another pub along the way gave us a sheep's head, so we bought some carrots, onions and swedes in the local shops and cooked up a tremendous Irish stew in our caravan. It was truly delicious, washed down with a pint of Guinness, and was much appreciated by the boys from Newcastle.

We ended up at one stage on the film set of a movie being made about King Alfred, with David Hemmings playing the king, where we spent a couple of days as extras, and were very impressed at how much money we could make, standing around, doing nothing.

During our second week Lulu and I then drove over to the West Coast of Ireland with a friend from London, Jimmy, an Irish Catholic, who insisted on stopping at every religious shrine on the way to get out and pray. We had booked into the medieval feast at Bunratty Castle, where a vast amount of mead (an ancient alcoholic drink made from honey) was consumed, and Lulu and I ended up dancing on the table, much to the horror of the very staid American tourists.

From there we were invited to go to a wedding with some young Irish farmers, and Lulu ended up falling into the River Shannon in her new Charles Jourdan shoes. The next day we took the wee ferry to the Aran Islands out of Galway town, where we trotted round in a horse and trap, completely entranced by the Irish people we met there, and everywhere else in Ireland.

Another shorter train trip on a Bank Holiday weekend that year was up to Scotland, where we attended the awesome Military Tattoo at Edinburgh Castle. The next day we went for the full tour of Holyrood House, as I wanted to see the famed bloodstains, still visible on the paving stones, of Mary Queen of Scot's secretary, David Rizzio, who was murdered there. I'm a big fan of Queen Mary, having read several books about her life, so all these marvellous manifestations of her history were just really exciting for me. We also took the train up to the little fishing village of Aberdeen, where Hessey had arranged for us to stay with some friends of hers there, and then on to stay with Scottie's family in the town of Gatehouse of Fleet.

Scottie was my cousin from New Zealand on my Dad's side and his Aunt and Uncle, Walter and Cath McCulloch, lived near the old McCulloch castle at Gatehouse of Fleet. We were made to feel very welcome, being the first of a long line of Thompson sisters to visit there. Walter's father, Sir Andrew McCulloch, was awarded the Croix de Chevalier and Legion of Honour and was wounded three times in World War 1, before becoming Aide de Camp to King George VI, and eventually the Governor General of Malta. Despite all this glory, Walter and Cath were very down to earth and lovely.

However, although this was all great fun, it didn't feel exciting enough to me and I wanted to do something different, as usual. We had been living in London for just under a year, and I felt we had become a bit bogged down in our jobs, even with the fun of our weekend excursions, and the couple of great holidays we had had in Scotland and Ireland. Sure, we loved the London way of life; the pubs at lunchtime and after work, and the fabulous boutiques in the King's Road, and the 60s clothes.

However, keep in mind that they didn't have the cheap flights to Europe in those days like they have now, which was why we hadn't ventured any further afield. It was Europe that really attracted me, so I started to scour the pages in *The Times* featuring jobs on the continent, looking for something new and interesting so that I could move over there.

I finally settled on a job I found in an advertisement in *The Times* for a Girl Groom in Germany, working for a Count and Countess Ortenburg in Bavaria. I applied, and got the job.

By then my second sister Robby had arrived in London, so Lulu would have a flatmate and I wouldn't feel too bad about leaving her there. I gave in my notice, and rather sadly finished up my job with Colonel Boehm, who, after all, really was a dear old stick, who bought me a large plaster cat from a very expensive shop in Bond Street as a leaving present.

At this stage I had arranged with Countess von Douglas to travel by train to Kitzbühel to take up her offer of babysitting her brother in this fabulous ski resort, before eventually continuing on to Bavaria to my new job as a girl groom with the Ortenburgs.

So, after a very happy (and fruitful) 10 months in London, I grabbed my skis and boots, and took the train to Kitzbühel, en route to Bavaria.

4. Adventures on the Continent

And so I set off into the complete unknown, hurtling across Europe in the train at night, clutching my skis and small suitcase, terrified I would fall asleep and miss my stop. As it was, I ended up in the middle of the night getting off the train, in Kitzbühel in Austria, and having absolutely no idea as to where I was supposed to be going.

The Countess had given me an address, and somehow, I found the apartment and had to wake up the 16-year-old brother and his friend, who weren't at all happy to see me. They didn't want anything to do with me or my babysitting ideas, so I very rarely saw them. To be honest, they seemed to be perfectly capable of taking care of themselves, and appeared to be very well behaved to boot.

I went off skiing the next day and that evening when I got back to the apartment there was this gorgeous man, another brother, Count Axel von Douglas – my new boyfriend! He was 6'4", blonde, rich, and divine. We fell madly in love and, quite frankly, carried on like a pair of teenagers.

We went skiing all day, every day, stopping at fabulous restaurants high up in the mountains, for beautiful lunches sitting out in the sun, drinking glühwein, and then going off 'tipsy skiing' again afterwards. Axel took me out for dinner every night, and then on to his favourite night clubs. It all seemed terribly romantic to me.

I discovered that skiing in Europe involved a lot more than actually 'skiing' - the social life was definitely an important part of the experience. I could never look at Mt Ruapehu, where I skied in New Zealand, with quite the same enthusiasm again.

Eventually, Axel had to leave to go back to Munich and asked me to go and stay with him at his apartment in Schwabing, the student quarter of Munich. By then my commitment to his sister, the Countess was terminated as the boys had gone home, so I drove up with Axel to Munich in his green BMW convertible.

I phoned Countess Ortenburg to explain that I was on my way, but was taking a brief sojourn in Munich, and Axel and I spent a wonderful few days, going out to lunch and dinner with his friends from the university he attended there. On these occasions I definitely felt a bit out of place, and didn't enjoy sharing him with the beautiful, classy, smart, multilingual, gorgeous women in the restaurants and clubs at night. They all spoke about four languages, and I could only speak English. However, I was possibly seen as being quite exotic, coming all the way from New Zealand. In the end, I know he became very frustrated with me, as I wasn't going to sleep with him, and it drove him mad. It was time to go to my new job in Bavaria.

And so ensued another long train journey up to the middle of nowhere, through dense pine forests, with everything covered in snow, to Schloss Ortenburg, the castle they lived in. It was right on the border with Czechoslovakia, which in those days was part of the Soviet Union. It is all quite different now, since the wall came down in 1989.

Graf (Count) Ortenburg met me at the station and drove me through even more pine trees to finally come out in front of the castle. It was like something out of a fairy tale, a massive old castle, surrounded by a huge courtyard bounded by high walls, and at the other end were the stables. I was terribly excited at the thought of living in a real live castle, albeit one with bullet holes in the walls.

The Nazis had appropriated the buildings at the beginning of the war, and Countess Ortenburg had been sent to a work camp for the duration, as she was related to the Dutch Royal family (enemies of Germany). Count O. was drafted into the German army. He was no big fan of Hitler but he didn't have a say in the matter – just like every other German man, he was sent to fight for Germany.

Eventually, American troops reappropriated the property, and there had obviously been a pitched battle at some point, as the many bullet holes in the walls and the general decrepit state of all the ground floor rooms attested. The rooms were enormous and cold and half empty, and my little room on the third floor had an open fire which was lit every night by Klara, the cook, bearing in mind it was now the middle of winter, and extremely cold.

This family may well have been wealthy before the war, and I know Count O's mother used to own another huge property in the North, but I ascertained they had lost everything during the terrible conflict that had raged around them.

There were marks on the walls where paintings had obviously hung, and the floors were devoid of carpeting or rugs. They lived a very frugal life, with the only sign of any landscaping surrounding the castle consisting of a huge vegetable garden where they grew all their own produce. In the winter all the fruit and potatoes were stored in the cellar, which was absolutely freezing – the perfect fridge. Klara was the only person working for them, and she was a lovely cheerful soul for me to have as a friend around the place.

The Countess was quite an aloof person, but Count O. was always very friendly, and he was very interested to hear about my Uncle Rob and my Dad, coming all the way to Europe from New Zealand to fight Hitler. He wasn't very forthcoming on any real details of his experiences during the war, but he was very thin and showed me photos of himself before the war when he was quite fat. In fact, he seemed to be perpetually hungry, and always finished everything on my plate. They were very fast eaters, and I always finished last, so I found it was just easier to not eat everything.

He fought right through to the end of the war, and, as he explained, anyone left alive in the German army was on starvation rations at the end. This is why, every Tuesday he made us a 'sheep stew' as he called it.

Germans are not traditionally very keen about mutton, and in the army they had to force themselves to eat it, by adding masses of gherkins, which is how he made it – it was actually quite palatable and tasty when he served it to us.

I very soon found out that working for these people was no picnic. I don't know what I had expected, but it certainly wasn't getting up at 5 o'clock every morning in the dark. It was the dead of winter and very cold, with snow everywhere and my first chore of the day was to light a small fire under the water tap outside the stables, to dislodge the ice in the pipes so I could water the horses and hose down their stalls. If I hadn't had Klara the cook waking me, I doubt that I would have got up at all.

I dressed every day in my oldest, warmest clothes, and after leading the horses into the indoor training area, I had to muck out the old straw and wheelbarrow it outside and replace it with fresh straw. Then I had to clean the horses, and feed them, (there were 14 ponies and Roger the stallion). For this I was paid the 'slave labour' wage of £5 a week. Finally, at 10 o'clock, after five hours' of hard work, I couldn't wait to go inside into the warm kitchen where Klara made me a big mug of hot milk with honey and rum. That was my breakfast.

Klara and I used to have 'tee mit rum' in the afternoons as well. She also made the best Späetzle (a German egg noodle pasta with a chewy dumpling-like texture), and her Apfelstrudel was out of this world. She didn't speak English and I didn't speak German, but we got on like a house on fire. She was my saviour.

After lunch I usually had the afternoon off, and I used this time to take Roger for a long ride every day. He was a devil, and many times bucked me off and galloped home without me, reins flying and me wandering along for hours behind him – rather like Honey! On the whole though I loved my afternoons off, although I was probably a bit lonely when I think about it.

One day I found a fabulous ploughed, dirt 'racetrack', stretching for miles which I decided would be a good place for a gallop. Apparently, I was very lucky not to get blown up, as when I was telling the Count about it later, he said that was the Russian border and where they had mines hidden. Another time, I found a nice, low, stone wall to jump, and ended up in a Jewish cemetery, where I had to wander around looking for the way out. Everywhere else was just millions of pine trees with dirt roads in between.

The Ortenburgs had two children, Franz and Nadine. Franz was 12, and about to go to boarding school, and Nadine would have been about 10. I took them to the swimming baths every Thursday night in the local town, driving the old Mercedes diesel car. On the weekends me and the kids would ski behind the car driven by the Count along the empty roads.

I went up to Munich a couple of weekends to stay with Axel, but that all became a bit fraught. I remember I used to hitchhike there, and on one occasion I was unceremoniously dumped out on the autobahn by a nasty truck driver who tried it on. I had insisted on getting out to avoid his unwanted attentions, and of course was immediately arrested by the highway Polizei and taken to the nearest bus depot and instructed to "take the bus" in no uncertain Germanic terms. There I was, dressed in my Princess Margaret tartan kilt, and matching cloak, long red boots, and little red suitcase – quite different from kids hitching today. I *always* got a ride.

I was definitely in two minds about my job with the Ortenburgs; on the one hand I loved working with the horses, and the relative freedom the job afforded me, but the work was very long and arduous, with not much in the way of appreciation being volunteered, particularly by the Countess.

So, I was pretty excited when Count O. invited me to go skiing in Wengen in Switzerland, while he took Franz to boarding school there. So I packed my skis in great excitement, acknowledging to myself that I actually couldn't wait to get back to civilisation again.

We spent the first night with his elderly mother who was living in a quaint 'gingerbread' cottage in the middle of the Black Forest, and on the way to Wengen we stayed in a very luxurious hotel in Wildhaus. Amazingly, I met up with my friends Trish and Marilyn from our waitressing days in New Zealand, who were working in the hotel as chambermaids. As was the norm, I had no idea they were even in that part of the world. They had gone there to ski but were always so tired from working, that they never had the energy to strap on their skis and get out there.

Count O. dropped Franz off at his school, which, judging by the buildings, looked very expensive, and we proceeded on to Wengen in the winch train, which was the only way to get up there. We were walking up the main street when I saw my sister, Robby, who I believed to be still in London, walking towards me. She had been working in a pub in London, and had come to Wengen with two friends, Kayebelle and Linda. I had no idea Robby was in Wengen, as in those days of no mobile phones, we relied on aerogrammes to keep in touch, so we basically never knew where anyone was on a day-to-day basis.

I knew Linda, from skiing with her in New Zealand, but had never met Kayebelle, who was from Melbourne and who was to become a very dear friend over the following years. Kiwis and Aussies were hitch-hiking and combi-vanning all over the place in the sixties, with little more than a place, date and time as to where to meet people. Somehow it usually worked out.

At this time, mid-winter at the start of 1969, the girls were working as extras on the Robert Redford movie, *Downhill Racer* and were being paid £7 a day! That beats £5 a week, in my money, so a change of career loomed. I approached Count O. and explained my predicament and he totally understood and was very nice about it and departed for home alone. God knows what the Countess thought. As I had spent the last three months working very hard for her, under rather 'frosty' circumstances, being paid peanuts, I justified my move by assuring myself I had got them through the worst part of the winter. They had managed before without me; they could do so again.

The girls invited me to move in with them in the little house they were renting in the town. I was very keen to start work with such a hefty pay rise in the offing, and the girls filled me in on the 'do's and don'ts' of extra work on skis.

One of the main things they had noticed was that more new extras were needed every day, so to be chosen on a daily basis, we needed to change our look, our ski jackets, and our hair do's to ensure we would be employed every morning. As we were all 'much of a muchness' size wise, we shared all our clothes and wore different hats, and did our hair differently every day, so we would look like brand new extras when we lined up each morning. Unfortunately for Robby she broke her ankle the next night as we slipped and slid down the icy path to our digs, which in those days was known as a Pensione. This necessitated a quick 'recce' to find a little sledge for her so that we could pull her along to parties.

This also signalled the end of Robby's employment on the ski slopes, and she was lucky enough to be offered a babysitting job with Robert Redford and his then wife Lola, taking care of their three young children, for the duration of the movie.

The Redfords were very friendly, and one afternoon they invited us all to a wine and cheese party at their very luxurious chalet, to drink the new 'green wine' Grüner Veltliner from the Tirol.

Robert Redford was still not really famous at that time, and this was the first movie that he had directed and starred in, and they certainly didn't put on any airs or graces. They were very hospitable, and there was no such thing as security surrounding them in those days.

Our very sophisticated friend, Kayebelle, was dating Gene Hackman, who she met at a party one night. He was also in the movie, but he wasn't so well known then either. We all thought he was a bit old for her, but he was a lovely guy and very friendly to all of us.

Linda, Kayebelle and I skied all day every day. This was the absolute best part of being an extra on a ski movie, as all your lift passes were free (normally a horrendous price). We Kiwis, (and one Aussie) soon got this lark sorted out. When you signed on in the morning, you were assigned to the First or Second Unit, and the appropriate passes were distributed. Most people then trudged off to stand around watching and waiting until they were needed.

Not us. Having ascertained in which restaurant the lunch was to be served that day, we simply took off skiing for the morning – absolute bliss. Sometimes we actually earned our £7 when we were roped in to 'tramp the piste' for the race scenes in the movie, working with the Second Unit at Wengen Alp. (Tramping the piste is spending hours stamping your skis to even out the snow on the racetrack: not an awful lot of fun, and usually on very steep slopes).

I had met a guy called Ginger who was a member of the Men's British Ski Team, and who was actually seriously skiing on the movie, and Robby has a photo of Ginger pouring champagne on my head for my 22nd birthday.

We may have skived off from tramping the piste, but we made sure we were around for the fabulous lunches every day in different restaurants, and we were also invited to a different party every night. According to another postcard home, there is a photo of me sitting next to Natalie Wood at someone's birthday party dinner. (Apparently, she worked as an assistant behind the scenes, typing script revisions, and shopping for wardrobe and props, and she also appeared, (well-disguised) as an extra, in some crowd scenes. Natalie Wood's then husband Richard Gregson was the producer of *Downhill Racer*.)

Years later when I went to see the movie I couldn't actually see us in any of the scenes, but a photo of me ended up in the advertising posters outside theatres. I am watching Robert Redford walking past me, and am in my pink ski jacket that I bought on my trip to Lech the year before. (That's me with my back to the camera. Some movie debut!)

We were all very sad when the movie was wound up, and we had to say goodbye to all the cool friends we had made over the past few weeks. However, as they say, all good things must come to an end, and that had certainly proved to be a very good thing.

We quickly transferred over to the James Bond movie, *On Her Majesty's Secret Service* that was also being shot in the same location, and we skied for a few days on that as well. So now we had to make some decisions as to what we wanted to do next. We all agreed we were big fans of the 'extra' way of life; standing around doing nothing and being paid for it definitely appealed, and if this 'work' happened to be in a great location, bring it on!

However, the Bond movie was about to move down to Portugal, so we agreed that I would fly to Lisbon, as I seemed to be the only one with any money. Strange that, as my £5 a week in Germany had not seemed so enticing at the time, but as it turned out, as there was nowhere to spend these riches, where I was working, I had probably saved a couple of hundred pounds. The girls were to follow on, hitch-hiking all the way.

5. I Fall in Love with Portugal and Spain

I arrived in Lisbon, once again with absolutely no idea where I was going to stay or what I was going to do, as seemed to be the case in so much of my wandering life so far. First things first, I needed lunch, so I found a wonderful-looking restaurant in the city and saw people ordering great steaming plates of wild asparagus. Not speaking a word of Portuguese, I pointed to this delicious looking dish and ordered it, and at the same time ordered a glass of wine. On that day I fell totally in love with Portuguese food, and the whole Spanish and Portuguese culture, and still feel that way today. I love their free-wheeling way of life, the food, the wine, the beautiful buildings, the culture, and the people.

A really good-looking, young Portuguese guy came up to my table and started chatting to me in English, which was very helpful, so I decided to enlist his help in finding me somewhere to stay. He told me his mother was a real-estate agent and had a little cottage out in the country which I could stay in for nothing until the other girls arrived. Talk about fall on your feet. He was very sweet and drove me out to this tiny cottage which became my home until the girls arrived about a week later. I guess I could have been a bit worried about staying way out in the countryside on my own, but of course I wasn't. Plus I had my young friend to come by on his motorbike every morning to take me into the nearest village for supplies, and to take me exploring. I suspect his mother had a good plan, using her handsome son to entice the ladies, and she would take care of our real estate requirements.

According to another one of my postcards home to my parents this same chap took me out to dinner at a "fantastic hotel 60 kilometres away on the south side of the river. At about 1 am we came back to the Van Gogh nightclub and danced till about 4 in the morning". Thank goodness for postcards, as I don't remember any of that. Also, I suspect that was the time he took me on his motorbike, something I wasn't about to tell my parents – no sense in them worrying any more about me than they already were.

In the meantime, his mother drove me around looking at houses for us to rent and we found a lovely old place in Cascais, about half an hour down the coast and close to where the Bond movie was filming the Casino scene in Estoril. The girls eventually arrived, but by then I had found out that in Portugal, all the movie extras are hired through modelling agencies – no wonder, as everyone there is so good-looking. So that left us out in the cold as far as the movie was concerned. What to do?

We spent a few days walking around the lovely old streets of Cascais, taking in the ancient buildings, and seeking out the cheaper cafés where the locals hung out. But as it was still early spring in Europe, the beaches didn't really appeal. I would have loved to spend more time exploring Lisbon, but we were now living over half an hour away from the city, so we amused ourselves by hitch-hiking over to Estoril, to ogle all the rich people and marvel at the Casino there, which is its main attraction.

As for making up our minds about what to do next, Linda and Kayebelle mentioned that they had heard that everyone was heading for the 'party town' of Sitges on the Costa Brava in Spain, so that sort of made the decision for us. 'Party town' a good ring to it, so we split into two groups, me and Kayebelle, and Linda and Robby, and set off hitch-hiking around the south coast.

A couple of hours into our trip, Kayebelle discovered she had left her passport back at our Pension. Damn! So we phoned the owner, who told us to make our way up to the border crossing into Spain, and it would be sent there for us to collect. This was so kind of them. I guess they realised we were travelling quite slowly with the necessity of hitching a ride each time!

Upon reaching the Portuguese/Spanish border, way up in the hills, Kayebelle and I were invited to sit with the lone Guardia Civil on duty there, for the whole night until the border opened in the morning. He made us comfortable sitting in front of the blazing brazier where he was keeping his feet warm, and we also shared his chorizo sausage and bread, and a bottle of brandy, and his enormous oilskin cape.

Thankfully, the Courier Post arrived in the morning bearing Kayebelle's passport, and we were very soon off on our travels again. We continued on around the south coast, of Spain, encountering the generosity of the Spanish people, over and over again. I remember one time we were picked up by a Spanish family who insisted on taking us home for the night, to give us dinner and a bed, and many admonishments regarding the dangers of hitch-hiking. This they dispensed in Spanish and in broken English (as our Spanish was at a very basic level at that stage). What were we thinking getting into cars with unknown people? It was very dangerous. (muy, muy peligrosa!)

Next morning they took us to the train station and bought us train tickets, making us promise "no mas autostop" (no more hitch-hiking). We thanked them profusely, cashed in the tickets and were out on the road again within a few minutes – we found hitchhiking to be quite addictive.

We visited the Alhambra Palace in Granada, which is an extraordinary place, and spent the night with a family in the Barrio de Santiago, an adjacent locality, famous for its inhabited caves excavated in the mountainside, dating back to the 16th century, in the town of Guadix.

There are about 2000 caves that have been used as homes for generations, and it is fascinating to see people just disappearing underground to enter their houses. We had dinner with the family, and slept in this beautiful 'cave room', and in the morning were awakened by tinkling bells out in the street. We stood on our bed and looked out the tiny window just above street level, to see our hostess hefting a big white jug, buying milk from the goats being driven down the road.

And so we finally arrived in 'party town'. Sitges was everything it had been cracked up to be – it was the place to be in 1969, and the town was bursting with Yanks. My first impression of the American girls was their beautiful big white teeth and their big bottoms! They were all gorgeous looking, tanned, and confident, and had tons of money.

The town was a great crossroads for GIs, mercenaries, musicians, 'Eurotrash', drug dealers, gold smugglers, drinkers and party animals galore. I wanted to be part of it all, having never previously been attracted to actually 'fitting in' anywhere.

Sitges in those days was reached either by train from Barcelona or by a treacherous cliff road that has claimed many lives and vehicles over the years. Sitges had been a Roman tourist town in its day, and still has an old Roman wall. The whole town is also a national monument, and the buildings in the old town are all no more than four storeys high, by law, so as to retain the town's authenticity. It is still very beautiful, with lovely old houses and walled gardens, but in those days, we only had eyes for the bars (and the boys).

I met Warren Frazier in the Kentucky Bar, where they played Credence Clearwater Revival, day and night. Warren was very popular there, and everywhere as it turned out, as he insisted on buying round after round of drinks for everyone, which they all accepted. I thought this was a bit rude so I insisted on buying him a drink in return (Kiwi style) and we became lifelong friends.

Warren was an American from Georgia, the only man I ever met who was born in the most primitive place in America, the Okefenokee swamp. He had fought in the Korean War where he had a very bad jeep accident and was then recruited into the CIA. I have no idea what he was up to in Spain, but he was a tremendous character, and tremendous in size as well. He was also extremely generous, which I noticed people took advantage of. He had an apartment on the waterfront in Sitges, where later on in this story, Lulu and I tried on a pair of his shorts – Lulu in one leg and me in the other! Big lad.

Speaking of Lulu, at that stage I had had a letter from her. She was still living in London, but now announced she was coming to Spain, and would I meet her outside the Madrid Post Office at 10 o'clock on a certain date? Warren happened to be going to Madrid on that day (probably he wasn't) and offered to drive me up there, a good seven hour drive. When we arrived, there was Lulu, standing with her little suitcase outside the post-office, right on time. Oh the miracles of aerogramme communication!

We had a wonderful time in Madrid with Warren, as he knew the city well, having lived there for some time. We all got on so well we decided we should travel up to Stuttgart in Germany, where Warren had an apartment on the American Base there. So off we went on a 'roadie', loading up at the PX (this was the GI's supply store, known as the Post Exchange) at the American base in Madrid. We stocked up on huge bottles of vodka, and big bottles of V8 juice to make Bloody Marys for our breakfasts on the trip, and off we went in his old black Peugeot.

We drove across Spain, then up the coast to France and over to St Tropez, where we spent the night sleeping on the beach. I have a photo of us in our sleeping bags in the sand, with a roll of loo paper and a bottle of ready-mixed Bloody Marys. I also have a postcard I sent to my grandparents from there, in which I seemed to be innately proud of only having spent NZ$2.40 in two days. Try doing that in St Tropez today; you certainly can't get to the beach anymore!

From there we went on to Nice where we stayed in a Pensione, which was the 60s version of an Airbnb, cheap and cheerful. We then travelled on to Venice where we stayed out in Mestre (for the cheap accommodation) and walked all over Venice in the rain. Worth every minute of rain when you get your first glimpse of the Grand Canal – nothing quite so breath-taking for the pure audacity of it all. A massive river right outside the railroad station.

We eventually made it to Stuttgart to Warren's apartment, and on the first afternoon Warren decided to take us to the Officers' Club for a drink. As Lulu and I never wore shoes at that stage, (a Kiwi thing which people seemed to find a bit disconcerting I have to say) they wouldn't allow us through the front door, so we proceeded to climb in through the window, and sat on the floor while Warren bought us drinks from the bar.

We were soon surrounded by curious officers, the most interested, (and interesting) being Alexander Haig, the United States Army general who served as the United States Secretary of State under President Ronald Reagan and White House Chief of Staff under Presidents Richard Nixon and Gerald Ford – yes, *that* Alexander Haig. He came back with us to Warren's apartment, and we partied on. I do remember Lulu lying down in a puddle on the way back, with us all stepping over her, chatting away, unconcernedly.

We remained in Stuttgart for the next few days, mainly trawling the isles of the PX for goodies (mainly booze) which was so cheap there. We then drove all the way back down, to Sitges, taking the route through the amazing Italian tunnels on the autopistas, or motorways.

When we got back to Sitges I met up with some young Americans who had a 'combi' van and drove with them up to Pamplona for the running of the bulls, or Festival of San Fermin.

Curiously enough, on the journey up there, we were drinking in a roadside bar one afternoon when these two guys pulled up in a sports car, introducing themselves as Dan and Mike. Unbeknownst to me, they were Tom's best friends, who I was to get to know very well in the future.

I met Lulu and her friend, nicknamed 'Aussie' as arranged, in Pamplona. (Don't even start to ask me how we met up with each other with no phones – I couldn't even do that in Auckland now). They had a tent in the campground, and dear old Aussie was very solicitous of Lulu and looked after her like a mother hen – mind you – someone had to, and I wasn't much use.

By the time we left Pamplona a week later we had black teeth, black tongues and black lips from drinking so much red wine all day and night from our recently purchased 'botas' (Spanish wineskins that you sling over your shoulder). Aussie made us hard-boiled eggs every morning for breakfast and went everywhere with a big black umbrella for some reason. He was arrested at the railway station for trying to kiss Lulu goodbye. Also, guys were being arrested for not wearing a shirt in those days in Franco's Spain. The Guardia Civil were very active during Franco's regime, and they came down very hard on 'extranjeros' or foreigners in particular. Aussie was arrested and he got a telling off, after which they told him to leave town.

Pamplona is famous all over the world and young people come from near and far to participate in the massive party that takes place over the week, beginning 6 July, and has been broadcast on Spanish TV for over 40 years. It was first discovered by the outside world, and written about by Ernest Hemingway in his 1926 book, *The Sun Also Rises.*

Girls weren't allowed to 'run the bulls' in those days, but we would follow the bulls down to the bullring and just walk brazenly in. Later in the afternoon, we walked back to the bullring and somehow always managed to get a seat, usually in the sun as those were the cheapest seats. I remember one amazing day when a very famous torero, Diego Puerta was fighting and he was so good he was awarded two ears and a tail, and someone threw a huge live goose into the ring, along with the usual rubber seats, hats and flowers.

Somehow, we got back from Pamplona alive and threw ourselves back into the Sitges lifestyle Ask anyone why they stayed so long in Sitges; it was usually because they would get so drunk every night that they would be too hung-over to catch the train out in the morning.

We met such characters as Pretty Tony and Bristol Bill, a couple of very cool English guys, very good-looking blondes, who seemed to be involved in smuggling illegal substances in and out of Turkey (mainly gold from what I could work out) and who used to get into all sorts of trouble.

Bill eventually was sent to jail in Portugal, I think it was for drugs this time and I visited him when I was there years later in the 1980s. He eventually died quite young from the drugs and the drink.

At this stage Robby, Linda and Kayebelle had left town, and I met up with an English girl, Susie Penry-Davy, a judge's daughter from Hastings. Susie was stunningly beautiful, tall with long blonde hair she could sit on, and was a big drinker. She had a ghastly American boyfriend who we all called Jelly Legs, who set his hair on fire one day lighting a barbecue at a party.

At this stage I was living on La Mumba's, (rum and chocolate milk) and my ankles started to swell up alarmingly from my vast alcohol intake. Susie's were the same, so our cure for this extraordinary ailment was to stand in knee-deep seawater every afternoon at the beach, drinking La Mumba's! Susie remained a good friend through everything that followed in my life.

So, we are now back at the stage that I met Tom, and left him after having dinner with him, as I had promised Gayle to travel to Corsica and Sardinia as arranged much earlier.

I had met a French doctor who was visiting Sitges, and he had invited me to stay with him in Nice, so that was where Gayle and I headed first. Hitchhiking in those days just involved a small suitcase and a bit of a show of leg on the highway. It was so easy to get a ride and always felt perfectly safe. We just went wherever the driver was going, got out, and hitched another ride. It was totally random, on the spot travelling and always fun.

So, Gayle and I continued with our original plan of hitch-hiking up to the Spanish border, and around the coast of southern France and, after a day in Nice checking out the ferries, we caught a boat to Corsica.

We actually had no real plans, just an ongoing wish to do something exciting and new.

According to another postcard sent to my parents from Nice (because, again, I don't remember this), I related how Gayle and I got a ride into France and along the coast to Avignon with a friend "in a 1969 Pontiac Grand Prix". Once in Nice I contacted Andre, the Doctor I had met in Spain, "who very kindly put us up in the Hotel Petit Louvre, for two nights and has been really wonderful". No wonder my parents were a bit worried at times. I'm a bit worried just reading it!

From there we set sail for Corsica, travelling 4th Class of course, as this was the cheapest way to travel when on trains or ferries in those days in Europe. It usually entailed sharing your train carriage with whole families spread around with all their attendant paraphernalia, including crying babies, chooks in cages and the odd goat or two. This could also sometimes entail sharing our meagre rations, with their delicious home-cooked tortillas, sausages and French bread – win win – for us.

When Gayle and I arrived in Corsica we decided to go on an 'economy diet' only eat when fed by someone else, which wasn't often, so our actual diet consisted of Corsican red wine and cans of sardines. Corsica was stunning, but we were keen to get on our way, and from Corsica we took a ferry to Sardinia and fronted up to this very posh-looking nightclub, *Pedro's*, right on the cliffs of the Costa Esmeralda, (the Emerald Coast). This whole area was owned by the Shah of Iran, better known as the Aga Khan, who had bought 'sight unseen' 70 hectares of this beautiful coastal stretch in northeast Sardinia and had set about developing it into an enclave for the rich and famous.

Tom had known the owner of the nightclub, Peter Kent, and his wife Carol, in Benidorm, where they had owned a similar type of club. What Gayle and I didn't realise was that they were all seriously into drugs, mainly cocaine.

Peter was an American, a very interesting character, quite enigmatic, very good looking and young for his age. He very agreeably found us jobs, looking after their boutique clothing shop by day and working in the nightclub by night, for our 'food and board'. He didn't need to worry about our accommodation as, after we had cleaned up the bar every night, we took our sleeping bags down the cliff to the beach and slept there.

However, Gayle and I just got on with our jobs, and even when we were asked to take over the bar (and all the cash coming into the tills) at night, we were treated as 'staff' by all the punters, which we didn't mind at all. A lot of the guests came from the Italian mainland and were obviously very wealthy, judging by the amount of jewellery being flashed around.

Interestingly, there was a Swedish guy living on the premises, Jurgen by name, who we weren't that fond of, and as it turned out, with good cause. The nightclub was situated within a big compound, which included the family living quarters and kitchen, with a huge courtyard. This courtyard contained rooms full of freezers filled with all the exotic foods Peter and Carol received from the mainland of Italy, brought over by friends, particularly from hunting trips. So there were freezers full of venison, wild boar, salmon, and all kinds of fish and game.

Our days were divine; beautiful place, beautiful people, water-skiing in the Mediterranean, and lunches in cliffside restaurants, (where I sampled my very first aubergine 'died and gone to heaven' cannot describe that experience). Peter and Carol were very generous, and always included us, during the day, in their long lunches of divine Italian food and wine.

At night, Gayle and I were very soon entrusted with taking all the money for the bar and cashing up at the end of the night, while Peter and Carol caroused the night away with their friends. Princess Margaret and her husband Tony (in England known as Antony Armstrong-Jones) came to the nightclub one night and, I sold her some clothes from our boutique. (This was my second meeting with the 'party' Princess, although I was gracious enough not to mention the time at the Victoria

League when I had met her in London – I figured she would have considered that to be a bit presumptuous of me)

There were also oodles of very wealthy and beautiful Italians wafting around, probably very famous on the mainland.

I'm sure that everyone who lived through this time has their own version of "where I was when Neil Armstrong and Buzz Aldrin landed on the moon on the 20th of July 1969", and mine is a great memory of constructing a fabulous couscous on a huge, round copper tray, complete with 'First Man on the Moon' written with almonds around the outside. As we sat down to eat this Moroccan feast, we craned our necks to watch the small black and white television with its grainy photos. It all seemed a bit surreal but exciting at the same time.

However, this fabulous lifestyle all came crashing to a halt one night, about three weeks after we had arrived, when we were raided by half a dozen members of the Italian police, the Carabinieri. The first we knew was all the lights and music went off, and next minute these thuggy-looking dudes came in with guns, smashed all the mirrors, and slashed all the cushions in the bar, looking for drugs. It turned out this Jurgen character had 'dobbed in his mates'. Peter and Carol and many of the punters were arrested and taken away in 'Black Marias" and the more well-known citizens quietly left, including Princess Margaret and Tony Armstrong-Jones.

All, that is, except Gayle and me and Peter and Carol's three children and, of course, Jurgen. The police asked us to look after the kids for the night, which turned into two weeks of house arrest for us.

To cut a long story short, Peter and Carol and several of their friends were sentenced to nine years in jail in Olbia, the capital of Sardinia. Gayle and I were taken to the police station every other day and grilled, about our reasons for being at the nightclub. There we were shown pictures of ourselves in the main Rome newspaper, which they threatened to send home to our families if we didn't tell them where the drugs were hidden. As if we knew!

We were also taken, under guard, with guns, to the supermarket each day to buy yoghurt and fruit for ourselves and the children. Eventually some relatives came from Rome to take the children, but we did all that out of our own pockets. The cops used to follow us out when we were hanging washing on the clothesline, hoping we would start digging up the drugs!

Back when the raid happened, the police cut the electricity at the gate, plunging the whole compound into darkness, so that was the end of power for us from that night on. This resulted in the freezers full of pigs and deer and salmon rotting big time, and every night I had dreams of all these animals and fish leaping out of the freezers and flopping around on the courtyard. I still think about it; the stench was *indescribable.*

I wrote to Tom care of the Dubliner Bar, Sitges, and told him of our predicament, and he replied immediately and said he had organised for a friend, another Tom, who had a yacht in Barcelona, to set sail to come and rescue us. However, we were under house arrest with no chance of escaping.

One day, totally out of the blue, we were finally taken to the police station and given our passports back and told to leave the country and never come back. Our first thought was to take our sleeping bags and go to a distant beach and sleep there for the night under the stars in freedom; so that is what we did. The next day we caught a ferry from Porto Cervo back to Barcelona and eventually back to Sitges and Tom.

6. Back to Sitges & Tom

I arrived back in Sitges to continue with my 'romance', by moving in with Tom straight away. I have to admit here that I was very nervous about it, as for me this was the real deal I thought, which would actually involve 'sex', something I had been astutely avoiding for several years now. And, it was my first real 'affair'.

I wasn't yet on the pill, so was instructed by Tom to go to the Pharmacia in the town square and ask for the 'anti-baby' pill which was dispensed to me over the counter - no questions asked. I just popped the pill in my mouth and presented myself to my lover, thinking that now all would just fall into place. I totally trusted him, and he treated me very gently and respectfully, so I was very happy about the whole 'huge' thing!

It didn't quite turn out like that. The first time we made love, which was that afternoon, I hyperventilated which, according to Dr Google can cause 'a fast heartbeat, tingling in the hands and feet, and fainting'. However, I didn't know any of that at the time – way before Dr Google had been thought of. Believe me, all of that happened, and also it prevented me from being able to speak and tell him what was wrong. So the poor man had to call his GP, Dr Cellis, who hastened around to our apartment behind the Dubliner Bar, took one look at me and instructed Tom to give me a dose of straight gin.

That seemed to do the trick, and after another brief fainting spell with horrible tingling hands, we experienced no more problems, and may I venture, never did again!

Tom's apartment consisted of an airy living room, leading on to a sunny terrace out the back, a tiny kitchen, two bedrooms and a bathroom. He had a maid called Maria, an older lady who came every day and took care of all the cleaning, laundry and shopping for essentials, all stuff that I came to realise Tom had never had to attend to in his life. And so, having known each other for approximately two days and one dinner, we began our life together.

Maria took a fairly dim view of me, 'tut-tutting" around me whenever she arrived, and I wasn't quite sure why she seemed to disapprove of me. Tom finally told me, it was because I wasn't pregnant, and I should be having a baby by now. I guess not being married might also have something to do with it. She kept up this 'playing charades' around me by pretending to nurse a baby in her arms. Quite soon after that she huffily told Tom she was quitting. I guess I was sort of stepping on her toes, keeping the place immaculate myself.

I had definitely ascertained that Tom was very fastidious, both with his appearance and with his surroundings, so I hastened to assure him I was perfectly capable of looking after the tiny flat. However, as we never ate in, he had no idea as to whether I could cook or not. Actually, I was quite proud of my culinary abilities, and had a battered copy of *The Robert Carrier Cookbook* as part of my travelling kit.

Now, I feel a bit of background is necessary at this stage to explain what Tom Corley was doing in a little bar and apartment in Spain. Tom was born in Dublin, Ireland, the second son of five boys: Jimmy, Tom, Joe, Philip and Ronnie. His father, Tom was an orphan who had been fostered out to a family in Northern Ireland when he was very young, where he was fed his dinner on the back step with the dogs.

He escaped from these awful people when he was only eleven years' old, and hitch-hiked barefoot to Dublin, and went to work for a tailor, working his way up eventually from rags to riches, and he ended up owning two clothing factories, making uniforms for the British army.

TP as Tom's father was by then known, was a very devout Catholic, and when he built their big house in Clontarf just north of Dublin City, he installed a grotto in the back garden, complete with a Virgin Mary and holy water from Lourdes. He was a wonderful man, very kind and gentle, and his wife Sadie was also a lovely woman and mother.

I had met Tom's other brother Philip and both appeared quite wild compared to their devout Catholic parents. The other sons were lovely, and lived a quieter life, all with their own businesses.

I know very little about Tom's younger life, as he was quite close-mouthed about his early years in Dublin, but he was very well educated, and his parents obviously afforded their boys a very comfortable and privileged life. Tom's mother had a 'companion' Betty, who also lived in their large house in the affluent coastal suburb of Clontarf. Apart from the fact that he told me how he hated his mother growing his golden locks down to his shoulders, I knew absolutely nothing more about his early years as a kid – he just never talked about it.

However, he did like to talk about the time in 1960, when he was about 23 when he sailed to New York to meet up with an Irish mate, Eugene. From what I can gather these two cut a bit of a swathe through the 'Big Apple', as only two Irishmen recently out of Ireland can. I know they joined the New York Athletic Club, to take advantage of the magnificent gym there, but mainly, they went to bars and drank.

One night on one of their famous piss-ups, having savaged several bars in Times Square, they fronted up to the Marine Corps enlistment centre there and signed on as marines. Having no memory of this whatsoever the next day, they were astonished and appalled to find the Provost Marshall banging on their door in the morning, ordering them to report to the Parris Island Recruit Depot immediately. Two very hungover Irishmen duly reported and spent an interesting year, during which they were involved in the infamous Bay of Pigs debacle.

Tom couldn't believe how much food there was, having arrived from post war Ireland, and, as he said, never having even seen a banana before. He told me he loved his stint in the Marine Corps, but could see Vietnam looming on the horizon, so he asked his father's doctor to send a letter saying his Dad was very ill and needed Tom to come home, so Tom was given compassionate leave to quit the Marine Corps and go back to Ireland. My son Nick is the very proud owner of Tom's Young Marine's Honour Graduate Ribbon.

At some stage after that he headed for the bright lights of London where, according to him, he was involved with the Kray twins and their nefarious hangers-on, part of the underbelly of London. Their gang, 'the Firm' committed murder, armed robbery, arson, protection, rackets and assaults between the late 1950s and 1967, when both were sentenced to life imprisonment.

At their peak in the 1960s they gained a certain measure of celebrity status by mixing with prominent members of London society, being photographed by David Bailey, and interviewed on television. When Tom decided to tell me about this rather seedy episode of his life, he also hastened to assure me that he was never actually involved with any of their underworld crime antics.

Tom's girlfriend at the time was one of Christine Keeler's mates, (I'm presuming here that everyone has heard of the Profumo Affair, involving Keeler, which rocked the political establishment in London during the sixties) and he kept a photo of her in his wallet, a beautiful black girl called Samantha.

They all spent a lot of time flying back and forth over to Paris to attend the races at Longchamp, which fostered his love for horse-racing and its attendant gambling, and which he later pursued with my horse-mad Dad when we visited New Zealand, many years' later. Tom had some very juicy, and frankly, almost unbelievable stories about his life in 'Swinging 60s' London, all of which I loved to hear, and swallowed without a query as to their veracity.

However, after subsequently living with him through the following ten years, I was more and more inclined to totally believe all of them – that was Tom; that was the way he lived. No holds barred – no Plan B.

I guess, because I was inured to his descriptions of his way of life in the past, I never stopped to question any of the things he got up to when we subsequently got together and were married. It never occurred to me that what he was doing was, if you like, wrong. It just all seemed like a tremendous lark, and I was always up for a lark. I had also frequently been told by my parents that in my general approach to life, I was like 'a bull at a gate' so we were a great pair.

However, he didn't tell me any of these shenanigans until we were quite a long way into our relationship, but I don't think it would have made any difference to me. I was caught, hook, line and sinker and I couldn't wait for the next instalment of our crazy life.

I never asked, nor was told, where all the money was coming from to fund his very decadent lifestyle in London and in Paris, mainly because it just didn't matter to me either way. That was Tom; that was the way he lived his life; don't ask.

This fabulous way of life came crashing down in 1967, when one night, according to Tom, he was involved in a fight with a guy in a bar in Newcastle in the North of England, which resulted in his dropping a slot-machine on a guy's head. Without waiting to find out what had happened to this person, he rang his father to ask his advice, who told him to get out of town as quickly as possible. And out of the country.

So Tom took his advice, and boarded a ferry to France and made his way down to Spain to the sleepy little town of Sitges, where absolutely nobody would know him, and waited for his father to turn up. Apparently, you could not be extradited from Spain to the United Kingdom until 1985. (Please bear in mind, I knew none of any of this when I first met him).

Tom quickly made friends with the most influential woman in Sitges in those days, Maria Teresa, who was the proprietor of the Bar Gustavo (named after her brother who had been killed in the Civil War) and she was also the most successful real estate agent in town.

When TP (Tom's father) arrived they recruited Maria Teresa to assist them in checking out various businesses and places to live, and settled on a newly built bar and accommodation in Calle Isla de Cuba, just off the main square at the top of town. This, then, was where Tom settled in to live, for the interim.

Tom then set about decorating the place in the style of an Irish pub, which became known as the Dubliner Bar, and eventually as a rather infamous hang-out of mercenaries and other doubtful types of person. It was also a huge hit with all the GI's and adventurers passing through town. TP went home, and since then Tom had been living relatively quietly.

And so, with neither of us really knowing anything about our respective upbringings, we embarked on the best love affair, for what seemed like forever. This mainly involved staying in bed all day, ordering pink champagne from *Els Pops* restaurant over the road, brought in by their lovely waiters in their long, white aprons and served to us in bed, and entertaining anyone who dropped by.

It soon became the party place to be, with people perched all over our bedroom, drinking, and eating gorgeous meals sent over from the restaurant on big platters, with Tom 'picking up the tab' every time.

Having never been a hedonist up until now, and understanding very little of what it took to be one, I jumped right on in and found myself enjoying this libidinous way of life. What had happened to little Penny Thompson from Manawahe? I guess she finally grew up.

We would eventually get up around 4 or 5 in the afternoon, and after showering and putting on some clothes, we would wander down to the Chez Swan bar on the waterfront where we would 'freshen up' with a few gin and tonics, before going out to dinner somewhere on the beach.

Chez Swan was one of the oldest foreign owned bars in Sitges, complete with crazy English bar owner, and a parrot in a cage, who only knew two words, 'fuck off', and is where I met the wonderful and infamous Bill Sykes. Bill's real name was James Thornton Sykes, and his nickname originated from the *Oliver Twist* character in Fagin's gang, a 'vicious robber and murderer', about as far away from our Bill Sykes as you could get.

Bill came from 'Bawston' (Boston) in Massachusetts in the United States and had been personally in charge of the Berlin Airlift immediately after the Second World War. He showed me letters addressed to him during this time – Bill Sykes, Berlin, Germany. That's how famous he was.

Bill had a serious drinking problem (you are probably thinking by now that everyone in Sitges had a serious drinking problem and you would be right). His friends, including Tom and Dan, took turns at looking out for him, and one afternoon Dan had locked him up in his Villa and taken the key, as Bill was too blind drunk to go out.

Not a problem to Bill, who, having set fire to the place by leaving a cigarette burning on his bed, somehow, climbed out a second storey window and ran off down the street yelling for the fire brigade. When they eventually arrived, Bill was nowhere to be found, but when he was discovered later, drinking in the Chez Swan he kept insisting, "Yo no fumo" (I don't smoke) to repeated questioning as to how the house had caught on fire. He was a dear, dear man, hugely intelligent and had married a pregnant German girl, Gisela, to smuggle her out of East Berlin.

In the meantime, our wonderful debauchery continued unabated for the next two weeks, until one afternoon, when Tom and I were sitting on beer crates in the back of the Kentucky Bar, and he was busy telling me he was thinking of flying up to Ireland to attend a friend's wedding in Cork. He then looked at me rather quizzically, and asked me, would I come with him? Not really thinking much about it, I said something flippant like, "I can't be wandering round the world with a man I'm not married to," so he said, "Marry me then". And I said yes.

I guess I should have taken this momentous decision I had just made a bit more seriously, but all I remember is feeling very happy and excited that my life with Tom was going to continue, and I never really thought about the fact that I had just said yes to someone who had asked me to marry him.

The actual fact of getting married to this virtual stranger never worried me. After all, two weeks and a couple of days would not normally constitute a proper 'getting to know you' period, but we were so comfortable together and never wanted to be apart for one minute, so it just felt 'right'.

Our engagement announcement then occasioned a very serious piss-up in the Dubliner, to which we invited Bill, and several of Tom's mates, who I didn't really know yet and who were obviously aghast at such a precipitous announcement. They had never seen Tom as 'the marrying kind'. From what I heard, people were actually quite shocked. When I think about it now, probably Tom was a bit shocked himself.

As for me, I didn't really have anyone to confide in, but I did phone my sister Robby in London to tell her, and for her to pass it on to our friends now all back in our old flat there, and I'm sure they were pretty shocked as well.

And, of course, I phoned my Mum and Dad. I didn't know what to say really, so I just blurted out, "I'm getting married!" My poor parents.

Here is Mum's version. They were sitting having morning tea at the farm, when the phone rang (so it must have been 10 o'clock at night in Spain). Mum answered and I blurted out that I was getting married, so, she quite naturally asked, "Who to dear?" Trying to describe Tom turned out to be an impossible ask, and after the initial shock they both poured a brandy and sat down to try to recover! Then Dad went back out farming.

All of a sudden we were thrown into action, and we had to make plans very quickly, as Tom's friend's wedding was the following week. Tom was to go on ahead to Ireland, and I was to fly up to London to buy some clothes. I was still wearing the clothes I had earned from my work in the boutique in Sardinia, which consisted of pairs of very swanky Indian cotton flares and tiny little fringed leather tops, with no bra. No doubt Tom was hoping I would buy some real clothes *and* a bra!

However, first I flew to Munich, where I had 'all my money" in the American Express office there. I had also promised to meet some friends at the Oktoberfest, which is held every year over September and October in Munich. I dutifully met my friends and managed one day at the Bierfest, then grabbed 'all my money', in other words, not very much) in travellers' cheques, before catching a flight to London.

American Express offices all over Europe were where many of us had our mail sent to, and sometimes we would pick up months' worth of letters and aerogrammes as well, our only connection to the rest of the world. How we ever kept in touch with each other, in hindsight, seems like a miracle.

7. Tom and I Get Married

Arriving back in London in September, just over a year after leaving there, I made my way to our old flat in Palace Gardens Terrace in Kensington, where Robby, Linda and Kayebelle were once again living. They decided to take me shopping in Kensington Church Street to the very popular and trendy boutique, Biba, where I bought a very 'mod' black trouser suit, the top part of which could also be worn as a dress (my wedding dress as it turned out). They also insisted on my buying a bra or two, and I also bought a pair of high black boots from Russell and Bromley. That was the full extent of my 'trousseau'.

I also visited a very up-market hair salon where I had my hair cut and streaked with blonde, which banished the wild and hippy look I had been sporting in Spain.

Our next stop was the King's Road where I fell in love with a beautiful full-length fox fur coat I spied in the window of another trendy boutique (I can assure you, buying furs was totally okay in those days). The girls attempted to prevent me from "throwing my money away" as they put it, but that only spurred me on, of course, and I went ahead and spent the £200 Mum and Dad had sent me as a wedding present on this beautiful fur coat.

I convinced Robby to come to Dublin with me to be my 'bridesmaid' so she dutifully also bought herself a black outfit, and flew over the day before our wedding. When I say 'dutifully' I don't mean I asked her to wear black. Like me, the smartest outfit she could find would have just happened to be black. Maybe it was the latest Mary Quant colour? I don't know, but one thing I do know is that my Mum and

Gran were horrified when they saw us in the wedding photos!

As this was probably the last time I would be staying at the flat, I made sure to pack up the rest of my belongings, which I had left there when I went off to live in Germany. I discovered I still had some really nice London clothes I could take with me, and also picked up my one other cookbook, *Robert Carrier's Great Dishes of the World.* Who knew, maybe one day I might be required to actually cook a meal!

When I arrived at Dublin airport Tom was there with his best friend, Terry Bent. Terry was very wealthy and had married the beautiful and wonderful Prudence, and had three sons, who all lived in a magnificent mansion on the outskirts of Dublin, where we were to stay. Tom had lined up his sister-in-law Isabel to take me shopping, as I patently wouldn't have any clothes that would be acceptable in Dublin.

Fabulously, I walked straight past them all in my new Biba outfit and high black boots, blonde sixties hairdo and full-length fox coat; he totally didn't recognise me. This certainly wasn't the girl he had kissed goodbye to in Sitges only a few days' before, so thankfully for me, there was no longer the requirement for me to go shopping with people I didn't know.

Having spent that first night at Terry and Prue's we all caught the train to Cork the next day, where Tom's friend's wedding was to take place. By the way, I didn't know the people who were getting married and I only met them the once at the wedding.

That night we checked into the Great Southern Hotel where we were booked in for the two nights, and on the second night I remember, after the wedding celebrations were over, we carried on back in the hotel in Rhodie and Nelly Bent's suite (Rhodie was Terry Bent's brother). They were dispensing delicious Sevruga caviar and champagne, and we were all having a wonderful time, when, sometime after midnight, Tom became agitated, (over what I don't know) and insisted we go back to our room, where he slammed the door behind us and punched me in the face.

This was so awful, and came so out of the blue, I just couldn't comprehend what had happened. In today's world, this is when I would have marched down the hall to tell his friends what he had done, and then left him.

Instead, all I felt was shame and guilt. I could only think I had done something terribly wrong, and therefore deserved to be hit. (I had taken a fair few hidings as a kid from my Dad, and they were always well deserved). A lot of booze had been drunk, and Tom proceeded to pass out at that stage.

Next morning, when he came to, he seemed horrified to see my black eye. It was as though he couldn't remember what had happened, so, incredibly, I went along with that, albeit with the help of a pair of big sixties sunglasses.

Just to be clear, this was the first and last time he hit me, at least for the next few years. Unfortunately, the abuse started up again when we went back to live in Sitges a few years' later, and really ramped up when we were living in the White House during our last few years' together, when he commenced to give me regular beatings whenever he was drunk, which was practically all the time.

So, we went on with unrelenting partying and drinking, and I loved every minute of it. We were in love and having a ball and without a care in the world – except we had no money.

We caught the train back to Dublin, and were married on the 2nd of October, 1969, a date I still quietly celebrate every year. I was 22 years' old.

We woke up that morning to snowflakes coming down the chimney in our huge bedroom in Terry and Prue's mansion. We filled the massive tub in our ensuite bathroom, and both hopped in, and Terry came up to join us with a cup of tea. Then he also got in the bath, and then Prue arrived with a tray of gin and tonics and kept us well lubricated, and great stories were told. Both men were smoking as well, so you can imagine the state of the bathwater.

Nobody seemed particularly fussed about the fact that we were getting married in the Dublin registry office at 11 o'clock that morning. It was just all very relaxed and happy, and once we had showered off after the bath, I decided to just tie my hair up with a green satin ribbon and don my black dress and boots. I then threw on my fox fur coat and I was ready. Robby had come over the day before to be my 'wing woman" and was staying with Tom's family, and we picked her up on the way.

We also had to stop off at Tom's older brother Jimmy's menswear shop in Dublin, where we had left Tom's only suit to be dry-cleaned the day before. Uh oh, Jim had forgotten all about it, so he very generously told his brother to select a new suit from the racks of very elegant grey suits, as he knew how fastidious Tom was about his clothes. Tom's youngest brother, Ronnie, in the meantime had gone off to buy me some flowers, and arrived back with an armful of white chrysanthemums, the standard funeral flower in Ireland!

We made it to the registry office with minutes to spare, where I was a bit shocked to see Tom's friends Squirrel Fitzsimons and Lord Richard Wrottesley casually smoking a joint outside the door. Inside the office they proceeded to pour us all a glass of Veuve Clicquot, much to the despair of the poor registrar.

It was at this stage we realised we didn't even have a wedding ring. Tom's third brother, Joe Corley, was there with his beautiful and vivacious wife, Isabel, and she took off her own wedding ring and gave it to me – for life! What a gal! When it came time to sign the register, I was shaking so much I had to kneel on the floor, and I still have the photo as proof of this.

We hitched a ride to our 'wedding breakfast" in the Guinness horse and buggy which just happened to be passing by outside the Registry Office, so I sent what I thought was a fabulous photo of us in the horse and buggy, home to Mum and Dad and my little sisters. However, Susie and Heather were devastated to see me, not in the white lace gown they had been envisaging, but in black, albeit with furs. Fifty four years on I remember every single minute of that day, and I don't regret a single one of them.

We all then proceeded to the Buttery, a famous cocktail bar in the Hibernian Hotel for more champagne, and then to the Shelbourne Hotel for an amazing wedding breakfast of caviar then steak tartare and lots more Veuve Clicquot. At some stage during lunch Tom and I realised that there was no way in the world we could pay for all this – there were 20 plus people at the table. Tom knew the Maître'd very well, from his 'wealthier days', and went off to negotiate a payment with him. However, as it turned out, several of Tom's friends attending had got together and had already paid for everything.

From there we all went off in different directions. For some reason I whizzed off with Lady Georgina Wrottesley in her E-type Jaguar to where she was staying in the Russell Hotel, to have a shower, wash my hair and change into jeans and boots. (Georgina was married to Lord Richard Wrottesley, a friend of Tom's friend Squirrel. This same Georgina Wrottesley was later to become 'infamous' as 'The Whip Lady of Marbella' in the Spanish town of that name).

Tom's parents, (who were not at the registry office, and who I still hadn't met) had finally 'come to the party' and decided to throw a wedding reception for us at the Howth Hotel. Up until then, they had totally refused to have anything to do with me, as I was a Protestant. Here, I am happy to report that they eventually came to like, and even love me, and we became very close friends, especially when my babies came along.

Apparently, they had invited around 100 people, friends and family, to this wedding reception, which was scheduled to start at 7 pm, but because we hadn't been told anything about it, until the late afternoon, we weren't really dressed for the occasion. We decided to turn up anyway.

So, at about 6.30 pm, Tom and Robby and I rocked up to the Howth

Hotel bar in our blue jeans and boots and ordered gin and tonics. "I'm sorry", said the barmaid, "we have a wedding on tonight and the bar is closed to punters." We tried to explain that we were actually the 'bride and groom' but to no avail, so we booked a room upstairs, and together with Robby, went up there and ordered drinks through room service.

So, all Tom's parents' friends had a massive wedding party without us. To this day I've no idea where they thought we were, or maybe, even cared!

In the meantime, Jo and Isabel had invited everyone up to their enormous house on the cliff at Howth to carry on partying, so we joined them all up there. Finally, some time after 1 o'clock Tom and I snuck away, and went on down the road to Rhodie and Nelly's cottage for our 'wedding night'. This little cottage used to belong to J.P. Donleavy, my all-time favourite author, and is where he wrote *The Ginger Man.*

Here, they proceeded to ply us with more bubbles until well after 2 am. Nellie had made up our wedding bed with red satin sheets, and next morning, there she was with a very welcome tray of gin and tonics. What a wedding day!

Now for the 'honeymoon from hell', from which we very nearly didn't come out alive. Tom's friend Squirrel was a very good friend of Lord and Lady Wrottesley (Richard and Georgina to you) who lived in England, but also owned a large stately home, Newtown House in Abbeyknockmoy, Co. Galway. Don't ask me why they had invited us to go and stay with them for the weekend, (or more pertinently, why we accepted) but it was all just a big adventure to me.

Richard drove us down in his famously elegant Facel Vega motor car which he was inordinately proud of, known, at the time, as 'For the Few Who Own the Finest', (and in which he was killed, aged 28 a year later).

It was about 8 o'clock at night when we got to this huge old house and were duly shown to our room. That was sort of it. No drinks, no dinner. They had a baby, Lord Wrottesley the 3rd, who was brought out by the nanny for our inspection, and who then disappeared again for the entire weekend. He was all dressed up like little Lord Fauntleroy in a blue satin suit, poor little lad.

We left Richard sitting in front of the open fire, in his rocking chair playing three-dimensional chess in his head – go figure. By this stage, even Tom was beginning to think we had made a big mistake. About midnight Lady W. started frantically knocking on our door, "Let me in, he's trying to kill me!" Tom responded by hauling a massive sideboard up against the door to block it, to stop them from getting in. Probably a good idea. It was all quite terrifying. We knew Richard had several firearms as he had proudly shown them to us.

We succeeded in surviving through the night, and in the morning I did a recce to the kitchen as we were starving. All I could find in the fridge was pâté de fois gras, smoked salmon, and caviar, and, of course champagne. However, we were eventually taken out in the land rover for a tour of the farm to get 'eggies' and to look at the beasties (cattle). All very strange. We had our eggies, then made up some unbelievable excuse that we had to go back to Dublin and asked Richard to drop us at the train station. I had never been so glad to leave anywhere.

We had a few more days of partying in Dublin with Prue and Terry et al, which included attending the races at the Currach, where I was shocked at the primitive conditions of the racecourse facilities, having been used to the Members' Bar at Ellerslie in New Zealand. They did have champagne and oysters though.

And so, we went back to Sitges. I was to discover that with Tom, there was no 'Plan B', so my life was to hurtle on apace.

Me at a party in Sitges.

My 22nd birthday in Wengen.

Movie theatre poster of *Downhill Racer* with Robert Redford and me.

Very early days in the Dubliner with Pretty Tony and Tom.

Not many photos *not* taken in a bar.

Kneeling to sign the registrar.

The bride and bridesmaid in black.

All dressed up behind the bar with Philip and Tom.

The Taming of the Shrew.

Winter in the Dubliner Bar with Philip, Mike and Dan.

Me, Tom, Sadie, TP, Susie Penry-Davies, Robby, Lindy, Kaybelle and Mike.

Philip and me with Scamp in Dublin.

Entrance hall of the Victoria.

Hotel Victoria
from the street.

Uncle Perry, friends and family in the Victoria.

Hotel Victoria back garden.

Alan with his Dad.

Guest room in the Victoria.

The infamous well in the garden at the Victoria.

Fred, Alan and Tom.

Party time at the Victoria.

Squirrel front and centre at the bar in the Victoria.

Pretty Tony, Squirrel, Major Mike, Scottish Freddy, Ovid, don't know.

The 'Boys' at the Capri Bar.

Philip's portrait of me.

Raphael and me at Nick's Christening in the Sitges Church.

Mac and Mardee with the boys at the beach.

Alan and me at the Casablanca.

Outside Ricky's with Robby and Mike.

Our 10th wedding anniversary.

The end of the beginning.

8. The End of The Summer of '69

The whole 'summer of '69' had led me to my meeting with Tom, and subsequently my life with him, but it also included for me the vibe of the '60s', the excitement of living in Europe at that time, as free as gypsies. We truly had not a care in the world, and we led our lives then as though we would live forever. We were a little bit wild, with no real care for our health (for a start we all drank too much) but we were also totally open to the next new experience; to anything that life could throw at us.

Meeting Tom certainly changed everything for me. It wasn't something I had been looking for, quite the opposite, as I had no intentions of 'settling down' to married life in New Zealand, or anywhere else for that matter. I guess you could say that the summer of 1969 was the catalyst for the rest of my life, and the very best part of that year was meeting Tom Corley.

I had never met a man like him before, and he absolutely fascinated me. He was just *so* his own man, and he didn't care who knew it. He was wonderfully kind and considerate to his family, and, eventually to my family too, and they all adored him. Although I was aware that he could at times be very difficult and hard-headed, the Tom I fell for was just lovely to me.

Looking back, I can see that these late summer months toward the end of 1969 were the golden times for us. We were so in love, I can honestly say that we just didn't need anyone else, and the incident at the hotel in Cork was easily forgotten.

We spent many long days up at the restaurant in the tiny township of San Miguel, drinking 25-peseta bottles of wine, and eating ensalada Catalana and chuletas de cordero (lamb chops on the grill, tiny and succulent). Taking advantage of the beautiful late autumn weather, we would also drive down the coast with some Dutch friends, to a famous fish restaurant right on the beach in Peniscola, where some scenes from *Ben Hur* were filmed.

On other long, lazy days Warren would drive us to the beautiful city of Valencia to one of the many paella restaurants that sat right out on the sand, with the sea rolling in around our feet, as we sampled various Spanish rosados and reds, while waiting for our seafood paella.

Autumn also signalled time for a visit up to Valls with Warren, a little town in the hills, to eat the fresh grilled baby leeks, 'puerros', with romesco sauce, wearing big white bibs to catch all the sauce dripping off the leeks, and incidentally our cheeks, and drinking red wine from the porrón, a traditional glass wine pitcher in Cataluña. You have to hold the porrón well above your lips to pour in the red wine from above, so that your lips don't touch it and you can pass the porrón on to someone else.

Winter by now was very nearly upon us, as the streets emptied out, and the Spanish people could begin to claim their town back from the summer hordes. Winters in Sitges were notoriously very quiet, as all the 'players' had gone south, and the regular tourists weren't due back until the summer. It was a particularly hard winter that year at the Dubliner Bar, with so few punters, and I have a photo of me, Tom and Philip, with Tom's buddies Mike and Dan, (the guys I had met on the way to Pamplona) sitting in the bar, the only people there. This was to be a regular occurrence throughout the winter, with very little money coming in.

With no money coming in from the bar, Tom used to play poker on a regular basis with some rich boys from Barcelona on the weekends. These were very serious games, taking place in the Dubliner Bar, lasting through the night till 4 and 5 in the morning. Mostly he won, sometimes he lost, and one never-to-be-forgotten night he came back into the apartment behind the bar, where I was sleeping. To my horror, he then proceeded to take out the deeds to the property, and put them on the table in front of the other players, to accompany the dozens of cheques for hundreds of thousands of pesetas already there. He won the hand, and the game, and kept the bar, but those bastards ripped up all their cheques. There was nothing he could do about it. I think he learned a lesson that night, to only ever play with cash.

I have been with Tom through scores of nights of very serious poker games and there is nothing more exciting, I have to say. I would inevitably eventually go to bed and wake up with him throwing piles of cash all over me. Then it was down to my favourite shop to buy a new fur coat or gorgeous dress. Sure, we had no money, but when he won at poker he always insisted that I buy myself something nice with the winnings. He must have lost some games, but he would insist on keeping on playing, sometimes until daybreak, to try to get his money back. These were very hedonistic times, albeit with very little money, and we lived them to the full.

Most Sunday mornings in the winter we would attend the bullfights. We would catch the train to Barcelona, usually with our American friend, Dan, to have lunch there and go to the bullfights in the afternoon. Dan was very knowledgeable about all things Spanish and induced me to read Ernest Hemingway's *Death in the Afternoon* so that I would understand more about the arcane history of bullfighting.

I have to admit to being fascinated by the whole rigamarole of the bullfighting world, and I read several other books on the subject, possibly to convince myself that it wasn't as cruel and horrible as it obviously looked. I was an unashamed animal lover, so for me to participate as a spectator in watching this barbaric practice was very out of character. But I did, and I really looked forward to our Sunday train trips to Barcelona, firstly to have lunch in one of the ancient restaurants surrounding the Plaza de Toros (bull ring).

I had fallen in love with the traditional Spanish style of eating, always beginning with a salad, or one of the multiple versions of the Ensalada Catalana. These consisted of crisp lettuce leaves with Spain's luscious tomatoes, red onions, roasted red capsicums, hard-boiled egg, tuna and salami, all drenched in olive oil, and mopped up with delicious Spanish bread. Still my absolute favourite.

Then, you would normally choose a seafood dish, again with multiple versions, followed by a hearty meat casserole or steak, finishing with a Crema Catalana, a creamy custard desert, very similar to the French crème brûlée. This lunch, of course would start with a chilled glass of Tio Pepe sherry, then a good bottle of the local red wine, would be brought to the table (there wasn't always a wine list – you enjoyed what was opened for you).

No lunch would be complete without the local 'carahillo de Ciento Tres'(translation too rude) but basically the truckdriver's drink, a short black coffee, with brandy from a bottle labelled 103. Depending on how much time you had, one of these could be consumed, or ten. Ten could be messy. They were very strong.

The corrida or bullfights began at 5 o'clock in the afternoon in the winter, so we needed to be at the bullring in plenty of time so as not to miss out on all the pageantry – and noise. Oh boy, were they noisy. Spanish music I believe must be the noisiest in the world.

One unforgettable day we were admitted to the 'holy of holies' the chapel beneath the bullring where the matadors go to pray before a fight. Seeing them there in the dim recesses of the chapel, so handsome in their beautiful 'suit of lights', that looked almost plastered on to them they were so tight, would make anyone's heart skip a beat. Certainly did it for me.

Out of interest, the term 'torero' is used for the lead fighter, and 'matador' for the rest. There were usually six bulls per fight, three matadors, two bulls each, so the fights didn't usually finish until well after 9 o'clock at night. If you were lucky you would be invited by a Spanish friend to the special restaurants where the steaks from the freshly killed bull were served – this only happened to us once or twice but it was a delicious and rather hedonistic experience.

Back to Dan. Dan was from South Carolina and was a draft dodger from the Vietnam War. He had very cleverly married a Spanish girl, Isobel. By marrying Isobel, in the Spanish custom Dan took her surname, so when the FBI came looking for him, there was no one with his name. Isobel owned a hairdresser's shop, where I had my hair and nails done every week, even when we had no money; it's a Spanish thing.

Not long after we came back from getting married, three American helicopter pilots came into the bar one night: one had lost an arm, one a leg and the third had obviously lost his mind, in Vietnam. This latter personage was to become a very dear friend, 'Lindy' as he was famously known.

Also, that same night another GI came in to play poker. His name was Mike Hidalgo, or 'Major Mike', the youngest ever major in the US army, who later married my sister Robby – a lovely guy. On this particular night, Tom threw them all out at 3 am, and told them to never come back, the usual carry-on. The next afternoon at 5, when we were opening up, Lindy leads the contingent up the stairs, waving a white flag, and we all became fast friends.

The one-armed GI brought me the LP of *Bridge Over Troubled Waters*, to join my record collection of one, Smetana's *The Moldau* which my old boyfriend Axel had given me in Munich. Tom only supported the playing of Frank Sinatra, at all times, and absolutely no other music was allowed, apart from a few Irish tunes in the bar.

Somehow we got through the winter, often spending afternoons in the Chez Swan by the fire, drinking and talking, and then walking back up to open the Dubliner, in our boots, jeans, and leather jackets, never seeing another soul on the way; there were even tumbleweeds rolling down the streets. It was so deserted and so different from Sitges in the summer.

At some stage, Tom started to behave very strangely, going off for days at a time, only coming home to shower and change, and then off drinking again somewhere. For some reason my response to this aberrant behaviour was to pathetically spend my time crying in our bedroom, until his brother, Philip told me to 'snap out of it'.

Again, something should have told me that this was not normal behaviour, but I was so innocent and *oh so naïve*, and I didn't want to face up to anything that might prick the bubble of our 'perfect' marriage.

So, I actually came up with quite a 'cunning plan', as Mr Bean would say. I decided to pack my suitcase, and clear all my stuff out of the bathroom, so that he would think I had left him, and I walked up the road to the Hotel Son Risa, carrying my little suitcase. The Son Risa was owned by some other Dutch friends of ours, Anna and Jack, two very colourful characters. Jack was gay and frequented the steam baths and saunas in Barcelona, with the unfortunate side-effect of his having to wear a towel tied like a nappy, at all times.

We had often been to lunch at the Hotel Son Risa, as Anna was an amazing cook and adored Tom, and for a start, when I arrived, she wouldn't hear a bad word about him. However, when I explained to her what had been going on for the last few weeks, she became more sympathetic, saying he must be experiencing a mid-life crisis or some such nonsense, at the grand old age of 33.

She succeeded in calming me with the reassuring words, "He'll come running, don't you worry". I found this interesting, as Anna, along with so many other people in the town, was, to put it mildly, astonished, that Tom had married this unknown girl from New Zealand with such alacrity. Apparently, he had never shown any interest in a long-term relationship with anyone before I turned up.

What happened was that he arrived back to our apartment that night to find me gone and, appropriately, was really worried that I might have packed up and left him. This was the whole idea as far as I was concerned, but I passed on a message through Philip to let him know where I was, and sat back to wait.

Anna was absolutely correct; a rather contrite Thomas arrived on our doorstep that night, with flowers for Anna and multiple kisses and expressions of remorse for me. It almost felt as though it was all worth it. I must say, we had a wonderful reunion, and he never did that again. Well, not for a very long time anyway.

Christmas came and went, which saw me cooking Christmas dinner for the few 'orphans' still left in town; two American guys, and Mike and Dan and Philip, and serving it out in the coolish winter sunshine on our back deck behind the bar.

We welcomed the sound of the church bells chiming the hour all day now, a sound normally drowned out by the music from the bars and the roar of the crowds in the street during the summer.

I was really enjoying these quiet times, as I had Tom all to myself, much of the time, and we had long talks about everything and nothing, as you do when you are just happy to be together. However, our lives were about to be turned upside down, and our relative peace shattered, never to be quite a the same again.

One day, early in the New Year, Tom received a very mysterious telegram from Ireland from a person who will remain unnamed, (let's just call him TJ) asking Tom to come to Barcelona and meet him in the Hotel Presidente. He had booked us a suite there to stay the night, so, without another thought, we hopped on the train (we didn't have a car) and went to meet the man who was to change our lives for the foreseeable future.

We took a taxi to this very swanky hotel, and made our way to the bar, where we told the concierge the name of the person we were there to meet. My first impression of TJ was of a very unprepossessing looking little man. However, we were to discover very quickly, that he possessed a huge, fertile, scheming brain. Why was he here? Apparently, he had heard of Tom in his previous life and his attendant business dealings in Dublin and London, and was here to 'make him an offer he couldn't refuse'.

The upshot was he wanted Tom to come to live in Dublin and become his partner in crime (he didn't say that, but that's how it turned out). When I look back on it now, it seems incredible that we would even consider leaving our beautiful life in Sitges and venture up to cold and drizzly Ireland, with absolutely no idea as to what was going on, nor as to how it would all turn out.

I guess Tom was very like me in some ways, in that we are both very impetuous and, impulsive, and always absolutely ready to grab on to any adventure and just go for it. Tom hadn't lived in his hometown for years, and we were very aware that we were moving to a city where we knew virtually nobody. Also, we had no money to speak of, so we wouldn't be able to buy a house or even a car. Off we went anyway.

TJ, as we called him, was a very ordinary looking fellow, who had never left Ireland at that stage, (except to fly to Spain to meet Tom) but he had an energy that matched Tom's and, as it turned out, they made a very good pair of crooks together.

TJ didn't believe in women having anything to do with business, which I was perfectly happy with. If it was in the least bit dodgy I didn't really want to know, but it all sounded very exciting. Tom was very enthusiastic about TJ and his plans, and couldn't wait to head up to Dublin to get started. I suspect by now that the quiet life in Sitges was beginning to pall, and he was keen to get back into the business of 'doing business'.

He was very excited to be on the move, telling me he wanted to show me the world (I think by then I had seen a lot more of it than he had), so we made our plans to leave the Dubliner in the dubiously safe hands of our new mate, Lindy, the helicopter pilot, who, over the next three years built up a very loyal following, and who eventually bought the bar from us.

We had no idea how long we would be living in Dublin, but when I left I made it quite clear to Tom, I wanted to come back to our beautiful little town of Sitges eventually.

As it turned out, we returned to Sitges three years' later, and in the ensuing years after that we spent many drunken hours with Lindy in the Dubliner Bar, including time with Warren Zevon, the musician, who wrote *Roland the Headless Thomson Gunner, Night-time in the Switching Yard* and *Lawyers, Guns and Money* with Lindy in that very bar.

Postscript to that story. Many years later Zevon was in Auckland, New Zealand, to give a concert, and I phoned the Intercontinental Hotel where he was staying and gave my name. Someone phoned back and said there were two tickets to his concert in the lobby for me. I took my friend Megan, and we went to the concert, although I didn't get to talk to him.

9. We Move to Ireland

So, now in the early spring of 1970 we were off to Dublin, again with no money. We had to stay for the first two months with Tom's parents, TP and Sadie, which was quite difficult for me, as Tom was out all day and many nights, plotting and planning god knows what with TJ.

Also, my relationship with TP and Sadie, to start with anyway, was not of the highest calibre. They were still very suspicious of my Protestantism, although it soon became apparent to them that I actually had no religion at all. We gradually settled into a genuinely loving relationship. They were both very good people, and I probably rather perplexed them.

With regard to the business that Tom and TJ got themselves into, to this day, I have never really known what they did, but it was basically selling non-existent gold to the newly oil-rich Arabs. Throughout the three years we were living in Dublin, we were either fabulously wealthy or dirt poor, nothing in-between, although TJ always seemed to have money hidden away somewhere.

I became used to these ups and downs, and I more or less just took them in my stride. We would get all excited about a deal going through, and then at the last minute something would go wrong, and they would have to start all over again. When a deal went south, first to go were the secretaries and next the cars; all the guys needed to keep the business going was the Telex machine, which was the only thing really necessary for their various nefarious purposes.

I was bored out of my brains, with no car and no money and set about looking for a house to rent, as quickly as I could. My lovely sister-in-law, Isabel, lent me her car and I found a beautiful old stone house over a weir out in the countryside, but Tom thought it was too far out of the city, even though I thought it was terribly romantic, and could see myself living there in the mill house over the water.

Finally, I found a cute little cottage in Sutton (between Dublin City and Howth) and we moved into 'The Chalet'. Terry's wife, Prue gave me a beautiful black and white cocker spaniel, Scamp, and I had a black cat who wandered up one day, whom I called Mr Keen. I was as happy as a clam. I was the picture of the perfect wife, cooking beautiful meals every night and waiting on Tom hand and foot.

He must have been both surprised and relieved that he had married a woman who loved to cook, and was actually quite good at it – ably assisted by my two Robert Carrier cookbooks. I loved cooking for Tom, but I also gave dinner parties for his parents, brothers and sisters-in-law, and eventually for friends we made along the way.

However, Tom was always happier when it was just the two of us, cuddling up cosily in our little cottage, with our animals and books, and enjoying a glass of good French red, I was certainly much happier than I had been to begin with in Ireland.

Once a month, on a Friday Sadie and Isabel and I would take the 'shopping train' to Belfast, as in those days, the prices of clothes and shoes up there were so much cheaper than in Southern Ireland. We would go shopping in all the big British stores and then repair for lunch to the Europa Hotel. This hotel was where most journalists covering the unrest in Northern Ireland hung out, and was known as Europe's most bombed hotel, earning the name the Hardboard Hotel. However, later on, when the bombs started, or, as the Irish insisted on calling it, 'The Troubles', we were forced to put a halt to our shopping trips.

This was a terrible time for Ireland. On 30 January 1972 the British Army had opened fire on unarmed citizens in Derry at a banned demonstration and thirteen people had died. Then there was 'Bloody Friday' on 21 July of that year, when the IRA retaliated leaving nine dead. The 'Shankhill Butchers' started torturing and killing Catholics, and then there was the retaliatory 'Bloody Monday' when the IRA killed another six paratroopers. The worst year for The Troubles was 1972, with 497 people killed and 4876 injured. No wonder we stopped taking the shopping train, to Northern Ireland – it became too dangerous.

Out of interest, two years' later when I was in Dublin on business from Spain, this happened. "Three days into the UWC strike, on 17 May 1974, two UVF teams from the Belfast and Mid-Ulster brigades detonated three no-warning car bombs in O'Connell Street in Dublin's city centre during the Friday evening rush hour, resulting in 26 deaths and close to 300 injuries. Ninety minutes later, a fourth car bomb exploded in Monaghan, killing another seven people. Nobody has ever been convicted of these attacks." These were terrible times, when the bombs found their way into our beautiful city of Dublin, and it certainly put me off going back up there for quite a while.

On to more prosaic matters. Most Fridays I would go into Dublin with Tom, and meet TJ's wife, Maura, who I was quite fond of. She was from the south of Ireland and even in the good times, her parents used to send her a parcel of bacon and sausages so she and the children wouldn't starve! TJ and Maura lived in a huge, very luxurious home in the poshest part of Dublin in Ranelagh, but were very down to earth and generous.

Maura would pick me up in her Mercedes convertible, which she asked me to drive in the city as she couldn't parallel park. She would insist on giving me a £100 note, as I didn't really have any spending money, and off we would go shopping (that was a lot of money in the 1970s, about £1,600 today). Then we would hustle over to The Buttery for a bottle of Veuve Clicquot, some oysters and lunch.

The guys would usually join us later and we inevitably ended up going out to dinner at one of the big hotels at the time; The Russell Hotel, the Shelbourne or the Hibernian, always spending like there was no tomorrow, with fantastical tips, so that we were extremely popular everywhere we showed up.

TJ loved pinching things out of these snooty restaurants and one night he even wheeled out an entire trolley with a bain-marie and Crêpes Suzette warmer still alight. Either nobody noticed, or for some reason, they never said a thing, and Norman, our driver, had to take all these things back in the morning every time.

We did a lot of outrageous spending. One Christmas, TJ decided to take a £1,000 in £100 notes into O'Connell Street, the main street of Dublin, and he and Tom started trying to hand the money out to people, wishing, "Merry Christmas" to all and sundry. People probably thought it was some sort of a scam, but a couple of savvy guys came by twice and pocketed £200 each of real money.

For reasons known only to him Tom never drove anywhere, and he had Norman pick him up every day to go to work and bring him home, which was a good half hour's drive each way. At this stage we had bought a car for me, an old Volkswagen, and I was thrilled at finally having the freedom to come and go independently.

Tom and TJ were away on the continent a lot, mainly in Switzerland and France, and sometimes I was invited to travel with Tom if he was on his own, but mostly he would bring me back bottles of *Joy* by Jean Patou, and beautiful French silk scarves to keep me happy. I was so happy anyway playing house with my animals, Scamp and Mr Keen, and looking after my man. If this sounds particularly galling to those feminists with their hard-won freedom from the male species, I don't apologise. I saw the way my Mum showed her love for my Dad and saw nothing wrong with slightly overdoing it with Tom.

We did go several times to Paris, staying in the Hotel Georges V, where Tom insisted on never leaving the hotel. I was keen to explore the Left Bank, but his idea of Paris was to take root in the best hotel, sleep there, and eat and drink there. I didn't mind too much at all.

We also had a wonderful week in Amsterdam, staying in the Hotel

Doelen, another beautiful old hotel, right on a canal. From there I could venture forth to the various museums where I could get my fill of Van Gogh paintings. I distinctly remember one night at the Doelen where we had a long dinner and meeting with a client, culminating in snifters of Remy Martin cognac. Tom and the client left me, at the table, as they needed to make some phone calls, and when they came back, all they could see was my fur coat on the chair – I was fast asleep under the table.

Tom's mate, Mike was now living in Belfast with my friend, Kayebelle, (yeah, yeah, small world I know). We had introduced them in Sitges and had attended their wedding in London in the Chelsea Registry Office the year before. They used to come down most weekends to stay with us in Dublin, as they were living in Belfast at the start of the Troubles and it wasn't a very pleasant place to live. I don't know what Kayebelle did there all day but she was very much in love with Mike, and he with her. Their marriage, however, ended very badly many years' later in Sydney, and I never saw the lovely Kayebelle again.

However, whenever they came to stay we always started with a wonderful breakfast on Saturday morning in the Chalet, of Irish smoked salmon and Veuve Clicquot, or Sevruga caviar, prepared with chopped hard-boiled eggs and finely chopped onion, and Melba toasts.

This was then followed by lunch down the road at Sutton House, the old Jameson's whiskey family home. Two beautiful Irish wolf hounds guarded the door of this very up-market hotel, as we sauntered into the lobby in jeans and boots, and proceeded to drink pre-lunch dry martinis, and the best of Bordeaux with our long, long lunches.

Another memorable adventure, while we were living in Dublin was the day we went out shark fishing with Rhodie and Nelly Bent. We had Mike and Kayebelle staying at the time, so Kayebelle and I got dressed in jeans and jumpers and met Nelly, who was all dressed up in '60s 'yachting gear', white pants-suit, high heeled shoes – she is a 'gas' woman. However, for shark fishing, you need to be a bit more realistic.

Rhodie and Nelly were horribly seasick and spent the entire trip in the toilet, spoiling their lovely outfits, as Kayebelle and I were kept busy baiting hooks with feathers, catching six mackerel at a time, for bait for the sharks. Tom kept us supplied with a steady diet of champers and wine and he and Mike were looking forward to catching the sharks. It was very, very rough out there in the Irish Sea and we never saw a single shark, but we had a brilliant time. Poor Rhodie and Nelly could do no justice to their huge hamper of smoked salmon, Sevruga caviar and Veuve.

I just had another memory of Dan visiting us in Dublin, I have no idea why, but he and I went to the Dáil Éireann (Irish Parliament). Apparently, we were there just before they put up the glass barricades so the public couldn't throw things at the politicians. We didn't see any throwing but observed a lot of bullshit and heard a lot of shouting.

We had a long-standing deal with Mike and Kayebelle to meet in Sitges every Easter, taking adjoining rooms in the Hotel Luna Playa on the back beach, with our other great mates, Fred and Maggie. Fred was from Germany and was one of the funniest men I have ever met, and Maggie was English and I had vaguely known her in the old days in Sitges.

The six of us would go on the biggest bender every Easter, drinking, eating, dancing, etc. Great times, and a welcome break from the dreary Irish weather for me. Don't get me wrong, I love Ireland and the Irish people, but living there, after having lived in Spain, was a wee bit boring, particularly food wise.

Back in Sutton in the Chalet, after dinner with Kayebelle and Mike one night, there was a knock on our door. Our cocker spaniel, Scamp, as usual was first to the door and, unsuspectingly, I opened it, to see a masked man pointing a pistol at me! Just totally terrifying.

Tom came to the door and somehow calmed this fellow down. He was IRA and had been sent to sort out the people in the car with the Belfast plates. They wanted to know why these people were visiting every weekend. We didn't really have a pertinent answer to that question, but managed to convince him they were our friends, one from Canada and one from Australia, so not trying to infiltrate the IRA branch in Sutton, had there been one. Most disconcerting.

During this time in Sutton, Tom's brother Philip came, inadvertently, to live with us, I guess so that we could look after him. When I think about it, we weren't that good at looking after *ourselves,* so I don't know what Tom's family thought we could achieve with Philip.

A few months' before, during one of our Easter trips to Sitges, we had been instructed by the Corley family to kidnap Philip and bring him back to Ireland to 'dry out' in the St John of Gods hospital, which was full of judges, doctors, and priests. Philip was a ferocious drinker and a giant of a man, with a wonderful head of red hair and a temper to match his formidable looks.

This kidnap plan proved trickier than you might think. He didn't know of our plans and was on a serious bender when we got there, and it took three days with all of us following him, to finally pin him down and get him on the plane back to Ireland.

In those days the Aer Lingus planes always went through Lourdes in France to pick up nuns and 'holy water'. Philip was still off his face when we boarded, and we were very lucky that he wasn't thrown off the plane, as he insisted on calling the nuns 'fecking penguins', and worse.

The whole Corley family were at Dublin airport to hustle him off to the hospital, and when they installed him there, he was given an injection which put him out for three days. He has never forgiven us for that. Philip and I didn't get on in those days, as he saw me as having stolen his favourite mate and beloved brother. We are great mates now.

However, when he was living with us it was, understandably, a bit of a nightmare for me, as he and Tom would have terrible physical fights, tearing the clothes off each other and trying to kill each other. Most of the time he would sleep all day and go out all night. If he forgot (or lost) his key, which was nearly always, he would bang on the door, then just smash through the front window to get in.

I also remember many nights coming out of our bedroom to find Philip, stark naked playing chess against himself at the table, or painting. Or one night I found him sitting on the floor in front of the fridge, eating the dog's raw calf liver.

Philip was, and still is, a very, very talented artist, who, when he was 15 years old, was the youngest person ever to be accepted into the Dublin Royal Academy of Art in 1962. Rather worryingly, at that young age, he was also a great drinking mate of Brendan Behan, the Irish poet and playwright and Irish Republican activist, and author of the worldwide best-seller *Borstal Boy.*

Philip went on to the Académie de Montparnasse in Paris, while living in the Military School there. He was at all times a bit of a handful, but a fabulous character and eventually a wonderful friend. At this stage, we were keen to get him painting and that is when he painted the portrait of me, which was less-than-flattering.

TJ had engaged him, to paint a mural in the children's room of their big new house, paying him a fortune, so Philip was ensconced over there for the interim and wouldn't let anyone view the work until it was finished. Finally, the children and TJ and Maura were allowed downstairs to see the finished mural. Apparently, it was so scary, the children ran screaming from the room and Philip had to paint it all over again, albeit, I presume, with fewer horrible monsters.

One night Tom and I came home from a dinner in town with TJ and Maura, and as we pulled into the driveway, we witnessed a thief staggering out of the house with our big TV set. Tom leapt out of the car, yelling obscenities, and the would-be robber dropped the TV and ran for the hills. Tom chased him for miles and came back with his beautiful suit all ripped to shreds. During these times Tom always wore very elegant suits, accessorised by a Patek Philippe watch, the gold cigarette lighter, you name it, and always looked amazing.

We had a great trip down to the Galway Oyster Festival one year with Mike and Kayebelle. We drove down in separate cars – at that stage we had a Jag – and we all stayed in a hotel in Galway and just drank Guinness and ate oysters all day Saturday. On the Sunday morning we had a few Bloody Marys to sober us up to drive home.

About an hour into the trip, we saw Mike and Kayebelle driving in the opposite direction, back to Galway, completely lost. We weren't faring much better, so we picked up this Canadian hitchhiker and got him to drive us home, as we were incapable of finding the way.

When we weren't going out and getting pissed in the most expensive hotels in town on a Friday night, Tom and I would spend a quiet evening with his antique dealer, John Callery of Callery Antiques. I loved those nights, sitting in the back of his shop, drinking a fine Bordeaux, and talking about paintings and furniture, and Tom's favourite, old cavalry swords and pistols.

We learned a lot from John and during the time we lived in Dublin, in good times and bad, we always set aside a portion of Tom's winnings (I would hesitate to call it a salary) to buy some exquisite pieces, which eventually ended up in the hotel we bought in Sitges, and later in our antique shop there. A stunning 19th century officer's military chest springs to mind.

I must have somehow made a good impression on TJ because on the 23rd of December in 1971, Tom arrived home very late at night and threw some airline tickets that TJ had bought for us, onto our bed. "We're going to New Zealand in the morning – wake me up at 6 am." I grabbed the tickets and looking at them, realised we were flying First Class around the world with Pan Am.

I didn't get any more sleep that night as I packed for both of us, and very early the next morning, woke up my lovely next-door neighbour, Cath, to ask her to look after Scamp and Mr Keen. I ordered a taxi and somehow managed to get Tom into it at 7 am and we caught the plane to London.

Once in London, rather than retire to the snooty First Class lounge, we opted to sit in the public bar in Heathrow airport for two hours; much more interesting, drinking and people-watching, and buying drinks for some American guy and for his stuffed duck. In those days First Class Pan Am had an upstairs lounge on the plane, where the pilots flew the plane and where you could have cocktails. Perfect for us, already pissed, before we even took off. It was an eventful flight in more ways than one.

Tom hates flying so he always must be drunk to get on a plane, so that when he finally passed out and went to sleep, he had a terrible hangover to wake up to in Los Angeles. I remember the lovely steward kneeling in the aisle entreating Tom to taste his specially concocted Bloody Mary to try to get him on his feet and off the plane.

As we went to transfer planes at LAX, we were arrested and taken to some room where we were interrogated as to why we had landed in the United States with no visas. Tom didn't tell them he had bribed the girl at the desk in London with a £100 note to enable us to board the plane without a visa.

There was hell to pay, mainly by Pan Am to the US government to the tune of US$10,000. On we went. At some stage in the flight, late at night I went up to the top lounge to find nobody flying the plane – I swear, there was no one in that cockpit. Also, at some stage I went to the loo, took off my emerald ring to wash my hands and left it there! Luckily not too many people were in First Class and I eventually realised it was missing, and retrieved it.

We hadn't had time to tell Mum and Dad that we were coming to New Zealand for Christmas, so when we arrived in Auckland, we got a taxi to my sister Robby's flat in Brighton Road in Parnell. We rang Mum and Dad from there and they drove straight in from the farm.

By now they had moved out of Manawahe and had bought a farm at Waiau Pa, about half an hour on the motorway out of Auckland. They were living in the original old farmhouse, but Mum had already planned her dream home, which, along with a swimming pool, would be situated right on the water there. It was perfect for them, and was a wonderful focal point for all their parties, daughters' weddings and a general meeting place for their rapidly expanding family.

It was pretty exciting as I hadn't seen them for four years. By now, it was Christmas day, so we went over to Gran and Poppa's in Takapuna for the usual Christmas celebrations and dinner, where my Gran pretended to not know who I was.

She was of the generation where people were at odds with either Catholics or Protestants (as I had experienced with Tom's parents in Dublin) and she was horrified by the fact that I had married, not just a Catholic, but an *Irish* Catholic. So, to say she was disappointed in me is a supreme understatement. I should also add here, she didn't have a religious bone in her body.

I probably wasn't too surprised when she said, "And who is this young lady?" when I got out of the car, and there was I, believing I was her favourite granddaughter. Tom charmed her of course and he spent a lot of time with my Poppa and found out that he had won two Military Crosses in World War I, which nobody in our family had ever been aware of.

I don't remember an awful lot about the rest of that holiday, as it was a bit of a whirlwind and we only stayed for two weeks. We went to the Ellerslie races a lot, as that is what my family did at that time of the year, and Dad and Tom became inseparable and went to the races in Wellington together as well – I wasn't invited. I just knew they would get on well and was perfectly happy for them to go off together, great old gambling and drinking mates that they were.

Also, at some stage Tom and I flew down to Whakatane where my godfather, Dave met us and drove us up to Manawahe so that Tom could see where I used to live. As Keith, Dad's farm manager had now taken over the old farm, he was happy to take us for a bit of a tour, and proceeded to drive us perilously close to the edge of the road 'up the hill' at the back of the farm. At one stage Tom was heard to observe, "Now I understand everything", as he clung, white-knuckled to the door handle. He never mentioned anything to me about that wee incident. Keith and I were smiling at each other.

When we left, we flew back through the States, without incident on the return trip and back to life in Ireland. It had been a totally unexpected and wonderful visit home. I was so excited for Tom to meet my family, and I knew they would love him – he could be an incredibly charming man when he wanted to be, and he seemed very happy to be in my homeland.

Early the next year 1972, TJ and Tom had to fly to Bangkok on business, and decided to take Maura and I with them and we were then all to continue on to New Zealand. Yippee for me! This started well, with First Class tickets all the way to New Zealand and back, but halfway through the flight to Bangkok Maura announced that she couldn't go any further as we were flying off the edge of the world. She had never been out of Ireland before, poor lady. So, when we got to Bangkok, I discovered that the New Zealand part of the journey was now off.

I tried to understand how Maura could really think we were flying off the edge of the world, as I knew she came from quite a poor background in the country, but did she really believe the world was flat? TJ wasn't much better, to be honest, and although he was the boss, as time went on, he proved himself to be a rather uneducated little man with boorish tendencies, and although I was fond of Maura, she was really quite ignorant of the ways of the world. As has often been observed, money doesn't always make for classy behaviour.

Tom wanted to take us on a tour of the nightspots, bars, brothels etc. having been there before in his previous life, but Maura wasn't having any of it. She wouldn't even go for a massage with me, "not from those chinks" as she so charmingly put it. So, neither of us could go. We could never eat any meals outside by the river because of Maura and the mozzies, and her unfortunately very sensitive Irish skin. She eventually took to her bed until we left.

Tom and TJ and I decided to visit all the Buddhas, and the traffic was so bad in Bangkok, that it took us a whole day to visit the Emerald Buddha, (without his clothes, amazing!), the Gold Buddha and the Lying Down Buddha.

The trip back wasn't particularly memorable until, TJ noticed me reading J.P. Donleavy's *The Onion Eaters* and took it away from me and tore it into shreds, saying it was seditious rubbish – as if *he* would know. I just bought another copy as soon as we arrived back in Dublin.

Many years' later when I was back living in New Zealand, I had written to JP Donleavy to tell him how much I loved his books, and that I had spent my wedding night in his cottage, and to my complete and utter amazement he wrote back to me. Thus began a wonderful correspondence which went on for several years and I still have a huge file of all his letters.

He was very amused at the story of my reading *The Onion Eaters* on the plane coming back from Bangkok when Tom's boss snatched it out of my hand and tore it up, much to my absolute fury.

The Ginger Man, which has sold over 45 million copies worldwide, had actually been both banned and burned when it was first published in Ireland. Coincidentally, JP told me that several people wanted to make a film of it, among them Robert Redford!

More strangeness. Tom and his mates used to know JP in Dublin all those years' ago, and were very suspicious of him, as he used to drink in the Buttery, and could be observed writing madly in a notebook, eavesdropping on their conversations, then translating them into his tales of a debauched Ireland.

JP was always threatening to come and stay with me on Great Barrier Island where I was living with my second husband, but eventually I believe he became quite ill and died at the ripe old age of 91 in 2017.

I guess I was starting to question our personal relationship with Tom and Maura, even though I knew that Tom's business relationship with TJ was paramount in our ultimate success. Also, I couldn't deny, that they were extremely generous and kind to us always. So, on we went!

In September 1972 I became pregnant with my first son, Alan. I had gone off the pill on the advice of my old-fashioned Irish gynaecologist and 'badda boom', pregnant! Once again, I really wasn't too fazed by it all, and just thought it was very exciting. I had never really thought about having children, and had certainly never discussed it with Tom at any stage. However, when I told him I had been advised to go off the pill, and what did he think about that, he was all for it. I would say we both thought it was very exciting.

A friend, Gill gave me a huge suitcase of beautiful pregnancy clothes – she spent a fortune on clothes and actually got married in Dublin Cathedral in suede hot-pants and boots, to the abiding horrified reaction of the 'high up' Dublin Catholics.

Tom and Maura gave us a beautiful white rocking cot from Paris with blue and white checked covers – I was in love with it. I didn't know then that I was having a boy though; it was a bit early for that sort of technology.

In the meantime, Tom and I were scheduled for a business trip to Hong Kong, so we flew out there and checked into the Mandarin Hotel where we stayed for six weeks, if you don't mind. We had very little money, but we had a ball. At night we would go out to one of the floating casinos and have a Chinese meal, and Tom would gamble. We very occasionally ate in the Mandarin Room at the top of the Hotel; beautiful food and hideously expensive but Tom's company was paying, so why not?

The best part of the hotel was the Oyster Bar down in the lobby, where we went every morning for Bloody Marys, not forgetting I was pregnant with Alan, but in those days my doctor had told me, "Not to change anything, to just do what you always do". It *was* the '70s.

In the middle of the Oyster Bar was a huge mountain of oysters on ice and the place was always full of expats and wealthy Chinese. I still have the cheque book from The People's Bank of China that Tom had been issued with from his meeting with the Chairman of that esteemed establishment.

We went to lots of shows and restaurants with our Chinese hosts, the head honchos of the Bank, and there was one occasion which I remember most vividly. We were seated at a banquet next to one of the most famous stars of Chinese Opera at that time.

Apparently, these young men are selected when they are very young (a bit like the Chinese ballet star in *Mao's Last Dancer,* Li Cunxin) and are rigorously trained and groomed for this spectacular brand of opera. His 'minder' and translator told us that they were basically starved and rigorously trained to do amazing gymnastics to strengthen their bodies so that they could wear the enormously heavy outfits, plus sing in these weird voices at the same time.

Also, their diet is just fish and rice and water for their whole lives, plus special herbs and supplements. Anyway, we sat beside this 'paragon of virtue' (they can never marry), and I observed he was dressed in a long black tunic and white tennis shoes. He was tiny, and endlessly fascinating to me. (I am writing this 50years' later and can remember every detail). He had two bodyguards, both carrying pistols, because, apparently, North Korea had kidnapped another Chinese opera star only recently, who had never been seen again.

The other thing I remember about these dinners and shows we went to was the unbelievable noise. Course after course of food, and whiskey (no wine) and terrible noise from the stage and the actual Chinese guests screaming at the tops of their voices, or so it seemed to me.

We also spent a lot of time in Macau, as Tom loved gambling in the casino there, and I remember a very old Chinese lady arriving at the poker table, apparently from mainland China, again with a couple of bodyguards. She then proceeded to fish hundreds of US dollars out of her bra and set to gambling with a vengeance.

We bought some beautiful pieces in the very old Chinese antique shops in Macau, and arranged to have them shipped back to Ireland, and they all eventually ended up in the Hotel Victoria that we bought when we returned in Sitges. We also loved all the gorgeous Portuguese restaurants and cute old-fashioned bars dotted around Macau.

When the time came to leave the Mandarin, TJ told us to leave most of our luggage in the room and 'do a runner' as he didn't have the money to pay for the room. So, I packed everything I could into my capacious makeup bag, and we went down to the reception desk with no luggage, to pretend we were going out for the day, and were astonishingly told that our bill had been paid. So, we hot footed it back to our room to pack. Maybe it was paid by the Chairman of the People's Bank of China? We will never know, but it felt a lot better than doing a runner.

10. Alan is Born & We Move Back to Sitges

Back home in Dublin, in early 1973, I remember I was very pissed off as Tom had arranged to go to Sitges for our annual get together with Mike and Kayebelle and Fred and Maggie, and I wasn't allowed to travel because I was too pregnant. However, the main reason he was going to Sitges was to buy the Victoria, as Tom had finally made enough money for us to get back to Spain, which had been our plan from the very start. How did these two men make this money? I honestly don't know to this day what Tom and TJ got up to, or how they made such big swathes of money.

Tom had asked Maria Teresa, our very favourite real estate agent and dear friend, and eventually the godmother of my second son Nick, to look for a 'magnificent mansion' as he put it, for our burgeoning family to live. She had dutifully found this beautiful old house in Calle Jesus, just off the town square, very run down, but it was being sold as a 'national monument' which meant we couldn't pull it down or alter the external structure in any way. This successfully put paid to the plans of any developers who may have had their eyes on it.

Tom and I were very keen to buy and live in an original Spanish home, and this lovely old 'mansion' sounded just perfect to me. In the end, we were the only people who wanted to buy it. I remember Tom mentioning to me how many 'hundreds of thousands' of pesetas the vendor wanted, and I was suitably horrified, but we trusted Maria Teresa, and the rest I left to Tom. I was beyond happy – we were really going back to Spain and we had a beautiful home to move into.

As you did in the '70s, I was given a date for my birth to be induced, on the 22nd of May, and told to be at Mt Carmel hospital in Dublin by 8 am. Tom arranged for a taxi to pick me up, as he didn't want anything to do with the whole business. I realise that doesn't put Tom in a very good light, in these present times when men have much more to do with their baby's birth and helping with the baby afterwards. In those days men very rarely witnessed the birth of their child, and certainly never changed them or fed them. Tom was just a typical man of his time, although most men did manage to drop their wife off at the hospital I have to admit.

I took the book I was currently reading, *Mila 18*, and read all day, as nothing seemed to be happening after I had the injection to induce. However, it was very disconcerting to hear women screaming down the corridor, and nobody came near me to explain the noise. I was busy trying not to seem too nervous, when I really was, all on my own, and I couldn't wait to finally have my baby.

Finally, around 6 pm the doctor examined me and found I was ready to have the baby immediately and rushed me in to have an epidural, but they never managed to get the needle in as I had Alan so quickly.

Seeing this perfect child lying in my arms was just so thrilling and unbelievable, I was almost crying. What an exquisite feeling to think he was all mine, to care for forever. Of course I phoned Tom as soon as I could (from the cute pink telephone in my room), and luckily I thought I knew where he would be, in the Bailey's pub in Duke Street.

Tom duly arrived at the hospital with French champagne and a whole lot of his friends. So, there I was, sitting up in bed, breast-feeding Alan, drinking champagne and having a ball. Alan was named Alan Thomas, Alan after my dad, and Thomas after Tom obviously.

Next day the barmen from the Shelbourne came in and set up a bar in my room for all the guests, who arrived in droves. Tom's youngest brother Ronnie installed himself as my private barman and sat there all day, drinking vodka. The nuns all thought he was my husband.

The Shelbourne waiters came every day and topped up all the liquor and wines, as unsurprisingly, I had lots of visitors who enjoyed a drink at the bar, as well as examining my beautiful baby. Tom and Philip would come in after eight o'clock every night with fabulous meals from the Shelbourne restaurant, and bottles of red wine and we would all party away.

I could have stayed there forever. As it turns out, I stayed there for a week. There was absolutely nothing wrong with me or my baby, but it certainly gave us ample time to bond and get the breast feeding and bathing down pat. Just as well, as I had nobody else around to help me once I got home. To be fair, I had already had a fair bit of practice on my youngest sisters (with the bathing part anyway!)

Next up was the great christening debacle. Tom's parents were determined that Alan Thomas would be christened a Catholic. I wasn't going to have him christened at all, so TJ came up with the idea of an ecumenical christening to be held in their new mansion. So, he hustled up the Catholic Bishop of Dublin, the Anglican Archbishop and a Jewish Rabbi. TJ and Maura invited all these guests I didn't know, who were instructed to bring George III silver as christening gifts. They bought the cake and even the christening gown, so they were made godparents.

I went off and bought a beautiful, long, pale green crepe Ossie Clarke dress with slits down the back and front to show off my new figure. I was downstairs at Tom and Maura's, feeding Alan, when Tom's mother, Sadie came in and said she would look after him for me for a bit. I didn't realise but they were so determined to have him christened a Catholic, that they immediately took him upstairs to the Catholic priest and he did the deed. Hilarious. Alan was christened in a beautiful George III silver rose bowl that TJ and Maura had given us. Unfortunately, all this fabulous silver got flogged off over the years when we needed money.

Six weeks after Alan was born, we moved back to Sitges. This move was hotly contested by TJ, who was furious with us for leaving, labelling us 'Mediterranean Swingers' for some obscure reason. However, we had finally pulled off 'the big one' and had close to a million pounds in the bank, at last, quite a bit in 1973, (£15 million today) and we were absolutely determined (well, *I* was) that we were going back to Spain.

What had happened a few months earlier, was we had pulled off a huge deal with the Arabs, which as usual I had no idea about. Tom and I were staying in the Mayfair Hotel in London, waiting for this deal to go through, as usual.

We were told the money was in the bank, so we went to Jack Barclay's down the road and bought a lime green Rolls Royce Cornice convertible and drove all round Mayfair in it. We came back to the hotel to find that our Arab agent, a diplomat based in London with a wife and family there, had completely disappeared with over three million pounds, leaving us completely in the dark as to his whereabouts. Even if I could remember his name, I couldn't repeat it here.

We were devastated, to say the least. This was our most trusted agent and he had left his whole family in London to fend for themselves. Personally, we weren't that happy about it, as we had to give the car back. Nobody ever heard from him again.

My fourth sister, Anna and her husband Stephen, were living in London at that time, and we had spent time at their cute two-storey cottage on the river in Windsor with them. We couldn't check out of the Mayfair Hotel because we didn't have enough money, so I gave Stephen my beautiful emerald and diamond ring, which he took down to Hatton Garden and sold. This only just paid for us to get out of our London hotel and go home to Ireland, once again broke.

Luckily, there was another deal in the pipeline and this time we got our associate Niall to go to Switzerland to pick up the 'goods' and finally we had our money (£1m) to leave. TJ was beside himself that we were leaving but I absolutely insisted. I had had enough of living in Dublin and couldn't wait to get back to Spain. To me, the whole exercise of going up to Dublin to go into business with TJ was to make enough money to buy a really beautiful home back in Sitges, and as far as I was concerned, we had accomplished that in three years, and I yearned for Spain.

So, we were finally on our way to Sitges. As we would be driving down through France and had no idea where we would stay on the way, I had to give my lovely dog Scamp to Tom's brother Ronnie, and Mr Keen, the cat, went to Cath, my next-door neighbour. We had a moving company pack up all our Waterford crystal and all of our antiques to ship down to our new life. Unfortunately, much of the Waterford crystal, which had all come from one of the christening guests, didn't make it. Some moving company!

Tom, for some unknown reason, bought a big, black, rather beaten-up Cadillac convertible to drive us down through France to Spain. What a wonderful trip! We had a Moses basket for Alan who slept in between my feet in the front .There were no seat belts in those days, or baby seats. I can't remember all the stops we made but one stands out in my mind, the Château D'Artigny in the Loire Valley near Tours. We rolled up in our battered Caddie to park alongside mainly Rolls Royces and Bentleys, and checked in to this rather posh establishment. We settled Alan down to sleep in our room and went down to the restaurant where Tom selected a bottle of Pomerol Château Petrus from the year of my birth, 1947. I doubt you could even buy that anymore, as it now selling between US$15,000 and US$25,000 today.

The cellar master became very excited, as we were surrounded by rich Americans who were drinking Coca Cola. He brought the precious bottle up from the cellar, actually covered with dust and cobwebs and decanted it into a plain decanter, over a candle in a silver candlestick. This was probably the one and only time we just had one bottle of wine with dinner, as it cost us £200, and Tom said, "We have to drink slowly."

We continued South through France and into Spain, and on to Sitges, and had to park the Caddie on the side of the main highway and get a taxi down to our accommodation, as the streets were too narrow for the car. We stayed in the Hotel Luna Playa for a few weeks until we got the Victoria habitable, at least enough for us to live in until we started doing it up.

The black Caddie convertible wouldn't fit down the streets of Sitges because it was too wide, so we left it up on the highway, and apart from a couple of excursions to the mountains, we never saw it again. The beautiful Victoria was in a very sad state, covered in dust and decaying leaves and rubbish, as it had been the beach house of a Barcelona family, who hadn't visited it for over 50 years.

It had several very valuable paintings on the walls, including a *Murillo.* Bartolomé Esteban Murillo, lived from 1618–1682 and was the most popular religious painter of 17th century Spain. His paintings being sold today frequently sell for millions of dollars. I mean, this painting was just *left on the wall*!

We employed a team of Spanish workers to clear away the many years' worth of detritus, and then we set about renovating it, to turn it into a hotel, with spectacular results. We moved into a couple of rooms upstairs on the second floor, one for Alan and one for us.

We had this great team of guys doing the renovations, with one young apprentice who couldn't have been more than 14 years old. The first day he was there, and they were having their breakfast at 9 am, I asked him if he would like a coke. "No, gracias Señora", he says, pulling his litre of red wine out of his satchel, the same as all the other workers on the team. They all brought their tortillas, sausages etc and ate very well for breakfast, before going home for lunch every day.

We built a huge new bar with a fabulous, blue-tiled front and polished wooden top, and pulled apart the whole kitchen, exposing the beautiful old white marble shelves of the former walk-in pantry. We also added a lovely wood-panelled dining-room with the requisite long wooden dining table and old Spanish sideboard. I had a lot of fun fossicking in Barcelona for antique Catalan plates and dishes to decorate my sideboard.

The Victoria had been built in the late 17th century as a private manor house, complete with high-walled garden and ancient well. All the indoor walls were covered in the most exquisite tiles, with the tiles in every room being completely different. The whole top storey (there were four storeys) consisted of a huge repository for extra tiles. Even the floors themselves were completely tiled in thick blue and cream tiles.

I loved my kitchen and painted it yellow. I would go on to paint all my kitchens yellow, as it is such a happy colour for me. Tom wouldn't hear of me cooking, so we engaged an American chef called Steve, actually a history professor, who was also a qualified chef. He was also a drunk and a complete disaster. I drew up the menu with him, but he was pie-eyed all the time and would disappear just as the dinner guests were arriving, so I ended up doing a great deal of the cooking anyway.

Pretty Tony, (actually his nickname, as he was very cute) from England was our barman, and when we opened the doors the first night, we had a massive party, with the women all looking pretty fabulous in our long dresses. Hilariously, some of the gentlemen attending from Barcelona thought they had been invited to an upper class bordello. From that day on it was basically 'open slather' in the bar, with everyone opting to have an account which they never bothered to pay. We also had an honesty book behind the bar for when there was nobody tending it, and it stayed open at the first page with not one name in it. Drinks, however seemed to disappear at an alarming rate.

My Uncle Perry, my mum's younger brother was an accountant in London, and he came to stay with us for a couple of weeks. He calculated we were losing 50,000 pesetas a day. He was horrified at our profligacy, but we had plenty of money and we really didn't care; we were having too much fun. We had huge parties out in the lovely garden at the back, with all the food and wine from our old friends from 'Els Pops' restaurant. It was a wonderful, marvellous life. There were undoubtedly many, many dramas – far too many to remember or recount here. Every day was just a huge adventure.

Tom flew up to Dublin on business, and for some inexplicable reason, left his friend Squirrel in charge of the hotel. Squirrel's first act was to throw my pregnant cat, Maria, down the well in the back garden. The well was over 60 feet deep, with rusted old iron steps down one side. Unfortunately, it was also our drinking water for the hotel. I strongly suspect that Tom had told Squirrel to get rid of the cat, so that was his way of 'pleasing' Tom. I wondered why he was poncing around the hotel the next day in his suit, with a red carnation in his lapel. It just sickened me.

So, off I went to the local Taverna to find someone to get the cat out of the well, and found a South African diver who agreed to climb down the very dangerous, rusty and disintegrating steps for 5000 pesetas, and got poor dead Maria out. I was furious with Squirrel and could have killed him, and duly reported his crime when Tom got back. However, he got his own back on me and told Tom I had made a pass at him. As if! Luckily Tom just totally didn't believe him and kicked his ass all over the hotel and out the door. Only temporarily, unfortunately.

Ricardo, our gardener, used to arrive every Sunday morning from his home up in the mountains, and would come in with some rabbits he had shot and make us a beautiful rabbit stew for lunch: oh the aromas wafting up the stairs, the scent of garlic and onions, red wine, and rabbit. One morning he left some fresh figs on the bar, and I helped myself and ate about four of them, not realising he hadn't yet washed them, and that they had been sprayed with DDT. I started to have violent stomach cramps and then terrific diarrhoea and then I started vomiting. Tom called the ubiquitous Dr Cellis, supposedly our family doctor, who called an ambulance, and I had my stomach pumped at the San Pedro de Ribas hospital. I mean, DDT?

One day when my Spanish maid didn't turn up as usual, I was mopping the beautiful black and white tiled floor of the Victoria entrance hallway, when a small but perfectly formed black man came through the door. I noticed he had a wooden fist tied around his neck, with the name 'Ovid'. "What's a beautiful woman like you doing mopping the floor?"

He insisted on taking over while I went to find Squirrel, who as usual had squirmed back into Tom's good books, and was living in one of our many rooms upstairs. Ovid had been in the Marine Corps in Vietnam with Squirrel and was one of the very few people who had a good opinion of him.

Tom was Squirrel's hero, and poor old Squirrel had followed Tom into the Marine Corps, without having a clue as to what he was meant to be doing there. So, that's how he ended up going to Vietnam.

Our helicopter pilot friend, Lindy continued to confound us with his crazy antics and one day he arrived in full Nazi uniform (he was six foot six) and proceeded to throw live grenades at the garden bar we had out the back, in front of our astounded and terrified guests.

Another time I remember we had a fire in the chimney. There were three open fireplaces, one on each floor, all connected by one chimney, which probably hadn't been swept for years. Well, the lower-floor one caught on fire. Somebody got Harold from the Chez Swan, for some reason, assuming he would know what to do. Harold tried blocking all the fireplaces with newspapers to deprive the fire of oxygen but that didn't work, so somebody else called the San Pedro fire brigade who, very embarrassingly for us, came down our tiny street and clomped inside with hoses and put the fire out.

However, none of these minor incidents can beat the terrible time when Alan got meningitis. I had been cooking all day for a big Sunday lunch; for some reason I remember it was a pork roast, and I had Alan in the kitchen in his 'Royal Family' pram given to us by TJ and Maura, which was later stolen by the gypsies. Alan started crying and acting up. This was unusual for him, and I thought he must be tired and needed some peace and quiet, so I took him up to his bedroom and put him down. He was very unsettled and wouldn't take a bottle and was crying, and having had diarrhea he became very dehydrated.

All I had was my trusty Dr Spock babies' book, which informed me that if he became really dehydrated, I should call the doctor. I had guests all sitting down for lunch, Tom half-pissed as usual and nobody to help me, so I called Dr Cellis who came around and said if the baby hadn't improved in a couple of hours to call him back again.

It was late afternoon when we could see that Alan was very sick, so we called Dr Cellis again, who came back around and immediately called an ambulance. It was just as well he did as Alan stopped breathing twice on the way into Barcelona to the children's hospital. I was totally wrung out with worry; how could this be happening to my beautiful boy? From out of nowhere my life was turned upside down, when something was occurring that I couldn't control any more. It was incredibly scary, but I felt so grateful for the ministrations and calming words coming from the wonderful medics, who kept Alan alive on that long drive into Barcelona.

You needed to take a big wad of cash to get into the hospital as there were no credit cards in those days. Also, in those days, as everyone had to pay to get into any hospital, so many just couldn't afford it.

When we got him in to the hospital and they had examined him, they said the dreaded word 'meningitis'. They did the lumbar puncture, which was horrific for the baby and for all of us watching,, and then told us to go home as he wasn't going to survive the night! Go home? Well, Tom went home.

That about describes his involvement with his children in a nutshell. I guess I was starting to understand that Tom lived his life, mainly for himself, and that anything to do with illness or hospitals was to be avoided, by him, at all costs. He just didn't want to be around anything like that. He also wasn't a very practical person, and left it to me every time to attend to all the necessary chores of life. I have to admit at this time, he was finding reasons to hit me, always drunk and at night, whenever I argued with him over something. I eventually learned not to argue with him.

In the hospital I lay on a bed all night with Alan in my arms, and asked the nurse for a bowl of water and a soft cloth. As he couldn't keep down any liquids, I just squeezed minute amounts of water into his mouth for the entire night. This seemed the natural thing to do as a mother.

When the Doctor came in the next morning, he couldn't believe that Alan was still alive. So, then they started administering drugs and I started to believe that he would live. I stayed there ten days with him, and Tom would visit every day with terrible stories from the local Spaniards in the village. So many of their children either died of meningitis or ended up blind or deaf or worse, which could have been due, in part, to the fact that none of them could afford to take their child to the hospital.

Well, we all know Alan today – there is nothing wrong with that man. However, it took him nearly a year to get over it – he was skin and bone and white as a sheet. I have a photo of him sitting on Tom's mother's knee out in the back garden. He looks terrible in that photo, so thin and white. So that was when he was ten months old and he went on to be a champion swimmer and triathlete, and an extremely healthy young man in mind and body.

In 1974 we made another trip to New Zealand. Once again we only stayed for two weeks, and that was the year that Dad's horse Blue Blood won both the New Zealand Telegraph Handicap *and* the Railway handicap sprint races. Tom put NZ$1000 on the nose on Blue Blood, in the Telegraph Handicap, resulting in huge celebrations in the Members' Bar at Ellerslie Racecourse in Auckland that day, when he came in first. Of course, that resulted in Tom shouting everyone in the Members' bar rounds of Veuve Clicquot.

We had asked Robby to come back to Spain with us as our babysitter for Alan. I remember leaving the farm at Waiau Pa and Tom was still so hung over from the night before when he crashed into the Christmas tree in the hall and swore at Gran, and we left him there on the floor for the night.

We were all in the taxi ready to go to the airport and my dear old Gran came out with a cold can of Steinlager in her hand and gave it to Tom. He loved her forever after that. However, his hangover was so bad that we had to get off the plane in Fiji and stay there for a couple of nights while he recovered in a darkened room.

By now I was completely used to this type of behaviour, but poor Robby must have been wondering what she had got herself into. We eventually got back on the plane and flew off to Mexico City.

Another memory of those times is that we were asked to hold a very secret dinner for the Spanish Royalists, which was arranged by the Count of Barcelona, who, at the time was the presumptive heir to the throne of Spain. This royalist faction had a bit of an underground movement going on behalf of the forgotten King Alfonso XIII, the last King of Spain, (the Count's father) who was alive and living in exile. Eventually, Alfonso's grandson, Juan Carlos became King of Spain, after Franco died in November 1975.

Not being aware of any of these machinations, we were told not to mention to a soul that the dinner was taking place in our home, and were asked to set 12 places for eleven diners and one for the exiled 'King' – right down to setting out the King's lobster and fillet steak, and finest red wine, (which we then removed and ate and drank in the kitchen).

I had been instructed to buy 12 dozen red carnations, for which they supplied a huge silver bowl, and they hung a cartoon of the King in his golfing clothes above his chair. It was all very hush hush and quite exciting. We could quite possibly have been shut down and taken off to jail if the authorities had stumbled upon this dastardly plot. And I shudder to think what might have happened to the plotters themselves. It was, in retrospect, a pretty hare-brained thing to do. However, at the time, it just seemed like fun.

11. Nicholas Comes Into the World

It was now early 1975, and we had only been living at the Victoria for just over a year, when one day a very wealthy Danish man arrived through the door and said he wanted to buy the hotel. He owned several spas in Germany and had fallen in love with the Victoria Hotel and just wanted to buy us out, 'lock, stock and two smoking barrels'. We had never considered selling, as we were so happy there, but we probably couldn't go on losing over 50,000 pesetas a day, in the bar alone, so we made up a really ridiculous sum of money and he hastened to draw up the papers and sign them, before we could change our minds!

We couldn't believe it, as it was three times' the amount we had previously paid for the place, including all our renovations. Also, we stipulated we wanted to take all our antiques out, which we did, and opened a beautiful antique shop behind the church to accommodate all our lovely stuff.

I must admit, I was terribly sad to say goodbye to our beautiful home, realising I would probably never live in such an exquisite and historic building ever again. Ah well, onwards and upwards seemed to be our mantra, and I was growing used to our lives changing 'at the drop of a hat' whenever Tom decided.

We then bought a brand-new apartment on the waterfront, on the fourth floor over Gustavo's Bar, owned by our friend, Maria Theresa. We went on to have such happy times there, luxuriating in our beautifully decorated apartment overlooking the sea, with Alan and I, in particular, taking in all the activity on the Paseo Maritimo, whilst sitting out on our fourth floor balcony. I would have quite happily remained there, at least for a while, until we found another house.

However, this was not to be, and before even six months had passed, Tom was out looking for some new acquisition or other. I think he just used to get bored.

We had by that stage bought the Bar Capri on the Calle Dos de Mayo, which was in the really touristy part of town. The Capri brought in truckloads of money, as it was always full of thirsty tourists, and was very capably run by our gay Spanish boys, Mario, Raphael and Paco.

On the subject of the Bar Capri, in the summer my job was to go down there every couple of hours and empty all the money out of the two tills and take it home in a suitcase. This wasn't because we didn't trust the boys; there was just too much cash coming into the tills and it was literally spilling out of the cash drawers.

That place rocked. I don't know why it was so popular, as Sitges wasn't 'the gay capital of Europe' in those days. All the punters were Poms, Irish, Dutch, German, Kiwis, Aussies, Yanks, all straight, but our 'girls' put on a terrific show for them every night and I guess it was, what we would now call, 'a point of difference'. Tom had a sign made for out on the front deck, in French and in English 'NO FRENCH'. This is because we were fed up with French kids who would arrive early and take the best tables, right on the street, order one coke and sit there all night. We wanted drinkers and we got them.

It is around this time, that I very excitedly and happily discovered I was pregnant with my second son, Nick, who I was convinced for some reason was going to be a girl – Nicola. So, having sold the lovely new apartment, we now rented a really old Spanish style, three-storey house at the bottom of town, rather run down, with the usual beautiful old tiles, and with very basic plumbing and electricity – the polar opposite to the brand new stylish apartment we had just left.

Tony Fix It was tasked with 'fixing' the very old candelabra in the main living room, and he had quite sensibly turned off the electricity at the mains, and was up the ladder trying to fix the light, when he received a massive shock which threw him on to the floor.

One of the 'foibles' if you like, of living in an old house in Spain, was that you had to keep a pair of Dutch clogs sitting underneath your various electrical appliances; for instance the toaster (very dangerous appliance) and the record-player. Even turning on an electric light could occasion a nasty tingling down your arm, if not a full-on electric shock. Warning guests against these potentially life-threatening appliances was an absolute necessity – and not just in that house either.

Now for one more of Tom's increasingly disastrous drinking sprees. He had been out drinking and playing poker with Lindy on someone's yacht and arrived home absolutely legless in the middle of the night. I remember it was pouring with rain and I was sleeping on the third floor of this rather dilapidated house, with Alan in his room, and heard this terrible noise of Tom crashing through the downstairs windows. He had arrived home with a TV under one arm (part of his poker winnings) and a Frankfurter in his mouth and had been pounding on the door to be let in, but I hadn't heard him, so he came through the windows.

Well, he sliced the main artery in his arm on the broken glass, and by the time I got downstairs, stark naked, pregnant with my second son, Nick, he was spurting blood six inches in the air, from his sliced-up arm, and was sitting in a pool of blood in a chair, vomiting up the Frankfurter – charming.

That night happened to be a fiesta in town, and with hundreds of people passing by on the street, who were staring through the window at the amazing sight of a nude, pregnant woman administering to a vomiting man covered in blood. *Nobody* offered to help (they *were* all tourists, not Spanish people), until, luckily our friend, Boss Henk came by and called the ambulance. In the meantime, I had made a tourniquet out of a tea-towel to stem the blood flow.

Apparently, when Tom finally got up to the hospital, they told him the tourniquet was so tight he nearly lost his arm. I stayed with Alan and someone went and told Robby and she came round to keep me company. Tom had caused all kinds of problems at the hospital and gave away his Breitling watch to the doctor for 'saving his life', which is what I thought *I* had done.

Tom arrived home about three hours later, by now 3 o'clock in the morning and insisted on going to the bar next door for a whiskey. Then Robby and I had to put him to bed. We had big leaks in the ceiling in the upstairs bedroom, and when we undressed Tom down to his white 'Marine Corps' boxers, we found little blood clots everywhere, where he had cut his bottom with the glass in the chair. Robby and I were in hysterics laughing, although, as I recall, he didn't think it was all that funny. How we ever got any sleep that night, hiding under the bedclothes from the leaks, is beyond me.

So, we then bought a beautiful old two-storey townhouse with a bar underneath which required a great deal of renovating. While this was occurring, we stayed in a very basic apartment across the tracks (the railroad ran through the middle of town) that Robby and Major Mike had just moved out of. Again, those are some of my happiest days. I was pregnant with Nick and content to just sit out on the roof terrace in the sun with Alan, and Robby would come around for lunch or a glass of wine. When the townhouse was ready for us, we moved into it and Tom was kept busy and happy doing up the new bar underneath, to be opened as *Raffles,* ceiling fans and all, as we had so loved the bar of that name in Singapore.

'Nicola' was due sometime in the New Year. I was so convinced I was having a girl (even though in 1975 we still had no way of knowing) that I had already named her after Edwina's daughter who had died in a car accident.

So here I need to introduce Edwina Hilton Jones. We met her when she first came into the Hotel Victoria. I guess in those days she was possibly in her early fifties (incredibly old to us then) but we thought she was very cool as she was beautiful and rich and cultured and she sort of became my mentor.

She had a gorgeous apartment over in Aiguadolć at the port, which was part of a new development up the coast from Sitges. We spent many very happy and, for me, illuminating, hours having lunches and dinners with her there. She was very elegant and worldly, and I wanted to learn all I could from someone like that.

We in turn, would invite her to *Mama's* in the port, our favourite new drinking spot, eponymously named after the lovely Spanish mama who owned and ran it. Here we would sit for hours, drinking banana daiquiris and eating *Mama's* exquisite food. Edwina told us a lot about herself, most of which I can't repeat here, as there were some *very* raunchy stories.

Edwina had been married to the head of ICI Spain, (Imperial Chemical Industries) there. She was originally from Wales but had a cultivated English accent and was obviously very well bred (pardon the term, but that was Edwina). She adored her husband and her mantra to me was, 'Don't make soup of your husband for your children; make soup of your children for your husband'. I got it, and still believe Edwina was right.

Tragically, two years' earlier, this wealthy, privileged family consisting of Nerys, their beautiful model daughter, and Nicola, and their sons, Gavin and Daryl, were on their way back to Barcelona after a skiing holiday in Andorra. Hilton Jones, Nicola and Daryl were in the family Mercedes car in front, and Edwina, Gavin and Nerys were following with a driver. Their following car came upon a terrible wreck halfway down the hill from San Miguel, with all three of their family dead in the wreck. Edwina never, ever got over it, but she stayed a brilliant and interesting woman for all the time I knew her.

I bought all her Irish linen sheets and lots of other beautiful bits and pieces she didn't have room for in her tiny apartment and we spent many happy days with her. Nerys was very cool, a Vogue model who used to stun people with her appearances in the Hotel Victoria. She also modelled for Salvador Dali, where he would daub paint all over her body and roll her onto a pre-prepared canvas.

My charming gynaecologist decided he didn't want to wait around for me to have my baby when he was going away for his Christmas break, so he made an appointment for me to be induced on 23 December 1975, as it turned out three weeks' too early. As usual, Tom couldn't be bothered to get out of bed for this occasion, so I caught a taxi at 6 am into Barcelona to the private maternity hospital. Apparently, in Spain, only prostitutes turn up to have a baby with no family to support them.

When I arrived, they stuck a needle in my arm and put me out, and when I woke up, my first thought was for my baby, 'Donde esta mi niña?' (Where is my baby girl?) It's a horrible way to have a baby, but I wasn't given any choice. Also, the shock of waking up and your baby has been taken away, with you knowing nothing about it.

So, I was told, "Your son has been taken to the children's hospital as he is very sick". So, I climbed off the bed, and they sent me in an ambulance to the children's hospital where they had Nick in an incubator with a collapsed lung, due to being induced far too early.

Tom had been phoned earlier to tell him to come to the maternity hospital to pick up Nick in his incubator, and take him to the children's hospital (once again, you must pay before you can get in). He and Mariano, our faithful taxi driver, drove up from Sitges to take Nick to hospital, while I was still out cold.

Once I got to the children's hospital Tom felt relieved of his duties and left to go back to Sitges. I couldn't even hold my new baby boy but stayed there for the next two nights, when he finally began to stabilise. I had to leave him there on Christmas morning, as Uncle Perry was arriving to stay with us, and we had various friends coming for Christmas dinner. Robby, as usual, was wonderful, looking after Alan, as I hustled around cooking Christmas dinner, for 10, while fretting about Nick back in the hospital.

I was so excited the next morning as the hospital phoned to say Nick could go home, so I once again took a taxi and left to collect this new baby boy. I was so grateful to everyone who had taken care of him, and saved his life, but after all he had already been through, I just wanted to take him home and cuddle him.

I don't think the world was quite ready for Nick. Well, I certainly wasn't as I thought that all babies were like Alan, good babies. Nick was such a totally different baby from Alan that I would have given him back, if there had been someone to give him back to. (Sorry Nick but you were, frankly, a handful).

From very early on he seemed determined to escape, so eventually, we had to get Tony Fix It to make a huge box for him in the children's room, so high that I sort of 'dropped' him in there at night and climbed in, standing on a small ladder, to get him out in the morning. This may sound a bit extreme, but without that box, he wouldn't be here today.

He was the ultimate 'Houdini', escaping at every chance he had. He definitely had the tables turned on him one day though when I brought him home in the 'royal family' pram. I used to have to take him out of the pram, take him upstairs, throw him in the box, (not really throw!) and then race back downstairs to get the pram and store it away in the hallway. This time, when I went back down, I saw some gypsies tearing down the street with it! I gave chase but they all laughed at me and I gave up. The royal family pram had done a Houdini.

Another of Nick's Houdini moves occurred out at the family farm on another one of our visits to New Zealand in 1976. Because of his predilection for escaping, the only place we could put him safely to sleep at night was underneath the desk in Mum's sewing-room, with a gate tied over it and the door to the room firmly closed. At last, I could sit down to a cool gin and tonic and relax and contemplate a meal with my family.

This reverie was cut short when my sixth and youngest sister, Heather thought she heard a splash coming from the direction of the swimming pool, and upon closer inspection, there was this nine-month-old monster, floating in the pool, having successfully untied the gate under the desk, climbed up onto the desk, opened the top window, dropped down into the rose garden and crawled around the house and into the pool. What to do?

Another time, as we sat watching him, he rode his trike into the pool and sat on it on the bottom. Mum was horrified when I ran to get my camera to take a photo of him happily sitting in the water.

On that trip we decided to take my fifth sister, Susie, with us back to Spain as babysitter to the boys, so on our journey back, we stopped in Sydney for a few days to visit Kayebelle and Mike who were now living in Elizabeth Bay. We were all tearing round getting ready to go out one day, when Alan, only two years' old, yelled out that Nick was trying to get out the window. We were 12 storeys up and Nick was working out how to jump out the window into the pool below. Enough already.

From Sydney we flew on to Rome and holed up in the Grand Hotel Palace on the Via Veneto, where Tom immediately took to his bed, hungover again. He told me to hire a limo to 'see the sights' so we did exactly that, and our lovely driver in his Mercedes limo took me and Susie and the kids to see all the sights of Rome. Then I asked him to take us somewhere for lunch where the taxi drivers would eat, where we had the best lunch ever, in a little hole in the wall that served pizzas.

That night, we hired a babysitter to watch over the boys and the three of us went to the *Sans Souci* restaurant and had the most amazing meal. We chose the Veal Saltimbocca Romana, a divine dish of veal rolled up with a slice of prosciutto and a sage leaf, braised in white wine.

We always had good fun with Tom when we were out, except, when on the many occasions he had drunk too much and was looking for trouble. We had a massive argument on the last night in the hotel, when he told me I could "fuck off" with my 'one-armed man socks'. I always used to sort out his clothes when they came back from the hotel laundry and mimic Mum folding Dad's socks, especially for a man with only one arm. It was the only way I knew, and still works for me to this day.

Back in Sitges, one of our favourite restaurants was La Masia up on the highway, which first opened in 1973. La Masia means 'the Farmhouse' in Catalan, and the speciality of the house was their sausage tree. Every table was presented with a gnarled grapevine set in a wooden stand, with various types of salamis and sausages hanging from it, say ten different kinds, to be nibbled on before our meal, all 'on the house'.

Well, this would have worked well with most people, but the GERMANS simply ate every sausage on the tree in one sitting, which was obviously not the idea. So, after a few months the sausage tree was taken off the table, which was very sad, but was totally the fault of the sausage eating Germans, most of whom were good friends of ours and we gave them heaps about it.

Right from the time when we had first arrived and bought the Hotel Victoria, we had joined the Club de Mar on the waterfront, as the only foreigners – somehow Tom got us into this bastion of wealthy Barcelona-ites. The Club de Mar had an Olympic-sized swimming pool where my kids learned to swim, by being thrown into the deep end by their swimming coach, Carmen, who would yell at me in Spanish, 'Leave! Leave! You don't want to see this!' No doubt indeed I didn't, but both boys became excellent swimmers, later competing in Triathlons in New Zealand, and Alan would become his secondary school swimming champ.

I would take them to the Club de Mar in the morning or meet the nanny/babysitter and they would spend the day there. They knew how to order their own drinks and go into the restaurant at lunchtime and order their own lunch in Spanish. By then, they both spoke fluent Catalan and Castellano, (the official language of Spain). They were great favourites of the two barmen there, Juan and Bonnie, and they literally had the place to themselves. In fact, I never saw any Spanish people there, and our family practically took it over, sunning ourselves on the terrace with a cold beer, before retreating into the shade of the poolside restaurant for lunch.

Although it was quite a snooty club, the bar and restaurant were decorated in a very simple manner, with red and white chequered tablecloths on the tables, and a typical Spanish menu. We always chose the Ensalada Catalana, (similar to a Niçoise salad) followed by a delicious fish of the day, prepared very simply and served with potatoes and green beans. The boys loved the food there.

The famous Fishermen's Bodega or Nameless Bodega on the back beach, was a great favourite for us after a really hard night out on the town. The fishermen would come in with their fresh catch of prawns and grill them with garlic and olive oil over the open fire. Oh, the fabulous aroma of those big crustaceans hitting the heat and sizzling on the grill, as their delicious juices flowed out, causing us to salivate while waiting for our 'breakfast'. We would join these guys in drinking rough red wine with our prawns, and fresh Spanish bread for breakfast, before staggering home to bed.

A woman remembers meeting me for the first time in that bodega when Lindy's wife, Lisa, had a fifth birthday party for Wolfe, their oldest son there. The Nameless Bodega had a garden out the back and, as usual, I wasn't interested in the birthday party, and had planned to drop Alan off at the party and go and meet Tom in a bar somewhere. This woman remembers me sweeping into the bar in my fox coat and high heeled boots, dropping Alan off and sweeping out again. She turned to Lisa and said, "Who's that snooty bitch?" I hate to admit it but I probably was.

When we left the Hotel Victoria we had far too many antiques to fit in our beautiful new modern apartment over the Gustavo's Bar, so we found the perfect spot for our antique shop, behind the church in one of the oldest parts of town, where there was a Roman wall. We painted all the walls of the shop in a beautiful sepia colour and brought in an antique desk and a fridge (for our drinks) and had heavy iron bars installed on all the big picture windows and the door. We hung our priceless Murillo and other paintings on the walls, and it looked really amazing. Tony Fix It made the necessary shelves and we soon had ourselves an antique shop – I can't even remember what we called it; in fact, it didn't have a name. However, it is still there, albeit in another iteration, selling small antiquities.

We loved that shop and did very well out of it. We would spend whole days in Barcelona, scouting through old antique shops and warehouses, and bringing back beautiful Spanish antiques to go with our Irish ones. I started out working there every morning, and I loved it, but Tom was always sending Tony over to tell me to lock up and come out to lunch, so eventually, we hired a Spanish friend, Raquel. She was very beautiful and did very well, and more importantly, was there every day, so she was a lifesaver.

One interesting event stands out. Raquel had a little 'moto' scooter and luckily always knew where we might be on any given afternoon, in one of the expensive, dark, and quiet restaurants on the waterfront. On this particular day she turned up at one of our favourite Spanish restaurants, El Greco, where we were lunching and said she just wanted to check the price of some Italian glassware we had on sale.

We had bought these six glasses for 500 pesetas and had them on sale for 1,000 for the set. She thought they were 1,000 pesetas each. She was just checking with us before she sold them for 6,000 pesetas to some Italians. Drinks all round!

The aforementioned gypsies (those who had stolen the royal family pram) were always coming round to the shop with stuff they had stolen out of old churches in the area. It was difficult to know what to do, as they often had some fabulous silver candelabra and candlesticks, which we would have killed for, but we had to turn them down, even knowing that they would find another buyer somewhere.

Another great antique shop story is when Tom bought two pistols from some crooks, who swore they were genuine Civil War guns.

We were assured they were 'originals' but we seriously doubted that they were – they were too cheap for one thing. Anyhow, one day, two Guardia Civil from Zaragoza came into the shop and expressed interest in them and eventually bought them. They wanted a 'certificado', which we didn't have so they paid for them, as far as I remember about 30,000 pesetas and off they went. Well, of course, when they got them back and showed them to an 'afficionado' of such weapons in Zaragoza, he could easily tell they were fake.

What we didn't know was that they had been assembled from the wood of old, burnt down houses up in the mountains behind Sitges, relics of the Civil War. They were then put together with odd bits of other pistols and buried in the ground, in vinegar to pit the iron and make them look old. Long story short, we had to pay back the 30,000 pesetas and apologise like mad in a formal letter and hope that it would all go away – which it did, as they also kept the pistols.

I should probably explain a bit more about what it was like living in Spain under Franco. I have researched and read a lot more since leaving Spain, about Franco and the Civil War, and in fact, I completed a Bachelor of Arts degree, majoring in History, including two papers on the Spanish Civil War. It was a vicious war, brother against brother, friend against friend, with terrible acts of violence and brutality perpetrated by both sides, and in the end the army, led by General Franco won. Franco was a Falangist, not a Fascist, although facilitating the bombing of Guernica and other cities by the German Luftwaffe remains a smear on his name forever.

This, from my history professor commenting on one of my essays: "Falangism has a disputed relationship with fascism, as some historians consider the Falange to be a fascist movement based on its fascist leanings during the early years.

"However, despite the links between Mussolini and the Falange, it is probably worth noting that the interests in Spain of Mussolini, and especially of Hitler, were essentially strategic rather than strictly speaking ideological. They wanted a new government in Spain to be beholden to them, and to be right-wing, but they weren't that fussed about it being fascist, especially as that didn't seem to be on the cards and would be resisted by Franco. They were therefore never really inclined to put pressure on Franco in favour of the Fascists."

We found living in Franco's Spain to be extremely peaceful and devoid of crime, at least where we were. My kids wandered all over the streets of Sitges when they were little, and I know I would not have allowed them to wander around the streets of Auckland in New Zealand, even in those days.

In fact, there was very little crime in Spain during that time, due in no small part to the presence of the Guardia Civil, locally known as the 'Toni Twins', as they went everywhere in pairs. (The real Toni Twins were the most photographed female identical twins in America and were, in their own weird way, quite famous). There was still a decent amount of opposition to the Guardia Civil as Franco's henchmen, and it was rumoured they went about in pairs as a safety measure.

Franco established these Guardia enclaves in every town, city and village in Spain to keep order, which tended to ensure there was very little corruption. Sure, the 'town police' could be corrupt, but the Guardia were supposedly 'incorruptible' as they were brought from other parts of Spain, and didn't fraternise with the locals. So, if you lived in Andalucía, your Guardia would come from, for example, Catalonia or Madrid. This meant they kept themselves to themselves, very rarely venturing out of their walled 'mini village'. Tom became great mates with Senor Roblez, the comandante of the Guardia in Sitges. He loved Scotch whiskey, so Tom always had a bottle on hand for when Roblez called in. The town police were very easily bribed and were easy-going townspeople for the most part.

My only real connection with the Guardia was during the Hotel Victoria years when we had tourists staying. I had to take their passports up to the Guardia enclave, the Ayuntamiento, every morning to have the passports stamped – I mean EVERY morning, without fail. You would only ever get a peek inside the doors, but they even had their own school going on up there. However, I can only presume that their señoras went to the market every morning, just like everyone else.

I guess a very good example of just how the Guardia Civil 'kept the peace' was one night, when we were all out late, drinking in Joe's Bar. This is where you went to drink when everywhere else was closed, so anything after 3 am. I remember we used to put our bags and things up on the bar, and we would drink or dance or whatever. Anyway, some stupid guy (we later found out he was Swedish), was so drunk he decided to swipe someone's purse from the top of the bar.

The Guardia were also in the bar having a drink and saw what he had done and chased him out the door. The next thing we heard was the Guardia shouting, "Alto, alto!" (Spanish for 'stop'). He didn't understand Spanish and kept on running and they shot him in the back – dead. It was incredibly shocking but that was quite a stark example of how they kept the crime rate down.

One of my real pleasures in my Sitges life was going to the market. I didn't go every day, as we basically went out to lunch and dinner most days, but I loved the market and listening to the señoras ordering their day's food requirements for the family. They would start off with the youngest little boy (girls didn't get the same treatment). A filet steak for the niño, then a sirloin for the señor and so on up the family tree to the grandmother who got the cheapest cut.

Intense and protracted conversations would ensue regarding the health of aunties and uncles and other members of the family, as usually in these families, they all lived together under one roof. It was quite natural to see the abuelo (grandfather) taking the children to and from school every day, and for the abuela (grandmother) to do the shopping in the market.

At some stage I had acquired a cute little green Deux Chevaux, a small, cheap French car variously named 'Rent a Dent' or, as my friend Daniel, who was Argentinian called it 'La Concha de la Lora' (translation unprintable, a vulgar Argentinian expression) green on the outside, brown on the inside.

I would drive to the market in this rather battered car of a Saturday morning and would buy up all the profusion of flowers in the market – my favourites being the gorgeous orange calendulas. I bought roses and irises and daisies and would take them all home to wherever I was living and spend the whole of Saturday morning putting them in vases and jugs and always had fresh flowers in the house. Mum had always had fresh flowers in the house, and I still love to do this, wherever I am living, even for instance, in an Airbnb in Italy.

Franco died in 1975, and we, and the rest of the world, were apparently kept 'in the dark' for about a week as the machinations were put in place for a seamless handover to King Juan Carlos, and a fully constitutional democracy. Elections were held and most people seemed happy with the result, as a law had been passed in 1947 allowing Franco to choose his successor, which we were all aware of.

Before Franco died, TJ had come over for some sinister reason as usual, and we flew up to Madrid and were guests at the huge walled compound where Franco and his ministers and friends all lived. There were hundreds of amazing, huge, modern mansions, with armed guards everywhere, and we visited one of them in a chauffeur driven car, but I don't remember much more about it, unfortunately. There was always just so much going on in our lives.

This was to be the pattern of our amazing life for five more years, never knowing what to expect next, what plans Tom had up his sleeve, but with me in love with him all the way. In all that time he only ever hit me when he was drunk, so that continued to happen on a regular basis.

Most people who lived with us, and around us, were aware of his not-so-occasional rages, and were smart enough to keep out of his way when he was drunk, but I seemed to be able to rile him up, more than anyone else. I thought I was just being cheeky, and often he would laugh at me, but it also far too often turned ugly, and I knew I had pushed him too far. I never, ever fought back as I knew he could really hurt me, if I did, so I just used to try to make myself scarce, or as a last resort, cover my head until his rage had abated.

12. The White House Years 1976–1980

About a year after Nick was born, Tom decided to buy the Casablanca, a bar and restaurant, with accommodation upstairs, near the Club de Mar in Sitges. It was owned by an English woman, Sheila who had run it as a business for many years. When we arrived to go over the property with her, she showed us how she kept all the half bottles of Coca Cola under the counter – something we didn't really need to be shown as we had been doing it for years. This is one of those strange facts that stick in your mind. Coca Cola was then more expensive than the vodka, rum and gin that we poured it into!

We now sold the three-storey townhouse and Raffles Bar underneath, and bought the Casablanca, as our new home and business. It was an attractive, white-washed building with green shutters and trim, divided into two, two-storey apartments with a large terrace restaurant out the front and a bar running down the side. We moved into the right-hand side of the building where there were two large bedrooms upstairs, ours with a balcony out the front and a bathroom. Downstairs was the maid's room, kitchen and living/dining room and another bathroom. The other side of the building we used as an indoor bar in the winter with accommodation upstairs for 'visiting firemen' (in other words, non-paying friends).

The floors of this rather modest building were all covered in stunning wine-red tiles, which our maid used to keep polished and gleaming to within an inch of their life. They were stunningly beautiful.

We hired an English couple, Steve and Babs – Steve as our manager and barman and Babs as one of our babysitters. We hired Pepe as another barman and sometime cook, with his dog, Blackie, and we also had Ann as a nanny and Aracelli as our maid. These started off as good times. The boys were by now old enough to go to the kindergarten in the village and eventually Alan would travel on the train to the American school at Casteldefells with the other kids of his age. Casteldefells was about 30 minutes up the coast towards Barcelona, and at that school the kids learned their lessons in English, with Spanish as their universal language in the playground.

As we could never have enough babysitters, due to our ridiculous social life, we agreed, at some stage, to hire Maria Teresa's cousin, Pilar, 'The Wart Lady' who was literally covered in warts from head to toe. Because of this unfortunate affliction she drank like a fish and was always stealing money to fund her habit. Maria Teresa thought if we paid her to babysit it might alleviate the drinking, and/or the stealing. Not so.

We went out every night for dinner anyway and always left either Ann or Babs or Joan, (three of many babysitters/nannies we had during that time) looking after the boys. So, we took on this unfortunate woman, who was probably in her late 30s, as one more babysitter. Things started to go missing, my camera, my fountain pen, money, and lots of booze. I began to hide things, and one night I hid all my precious French cheeses, that someone had recently brought me down from Andorra, in the washing machine, covering them over with clothes.

Alas, Ann arrived early the next morning and loaded up the washing machine with more clothes, and proceeded to wash all the cheeses as well. I arrived down to the kitchen to see squished cheeses and their French labels tumbling round and round in the machine amongst the children's clothes. Tom got a bit tired of this woman stealing and took her aside for a stern chat where she confessed everything and was instantly fired.

I was always taking in stray cats and dogs and one day a lovely honey-coloured dog arrived on our doorstep who I named 'Nova' after a flashy lifestyle magazine that had just started up in London. Nova turned out to be pregnant and very soon afterwards had nine puppies. I called the vet, Domingo and he came down and put four of them to sleep and we kept five, but she was obviously very upset about the disappearance of some of her puppies.

Gypsies were always knocking on the door trying to sell you stuff and this woman came by with some flowers to sell, (probably pinched) and Nova ran out and bit her on the leg. I gave her 1,000 pesetas which was a lot of money in those days and told her to buy herself some new stockings. As soon as her gang heard this they were back for more money, and then went to the cops when I refused to pay it.

The next thing I knew the town police in their Black Maria pulled up outside the Casablanca, and with all our punters at the bar watching, I was arrested with Nova and the five pups, and put in the back of the wagon and taken up to the court to answer charges. My Spanish was good enough to explain what had happened, that the dog wasn't mine and no, I didn't know if she had had a rabies inoculation. I got off with a stiff fine and we had to find our own way home – Tom was appalled and was no help whatsoever.

On to a more upbeat and artistic episode in our frenzied life, and one which I can relate, but can use no real names, as usual. We were friendly with a young Barcelona artist, whom we will call Francisco, through some mutual Spanish friends. One afternoon, during a drinking session in a bar somewhere in Barcelona we hit upon the 'brilliant' scheme of having Francisco paint a couple of Dali paintings and sign them with Dali's signature, and put them up for sale.

This took a few months, but eventually we were invited in to his studio to view the finished products. It was absolutely impossible to find fault with these perfect renditions of two of my favourite Dali paintings, *The Persistence of Memory* and *Gala and the Tigers.*

It didn't take us long to make the decision to take them up to Sotheby's in London to offer them for sale; they were that good. Tom made up some 'cock and bull' story at the auction rooms that we had discovered these masterpieces in an old warehouse in Barcelona, and having gone through Sotheby's exhaustive process of provenance research, to confirm their authenticity and historical context, they were accepted for sale.

Having made it through all Sotheby's Dali specialists, these fabulous 'works of art' were sold for a ridiculous amount, which was all very exciting, but we were sensible enough not to attempt something like that again. And on we went dreaming up schemes, or at least Tom did.

Tom was that type of person who needed to always be coming up with 'the next big thing' as far as making money was concerned. He would think up a really good scheme, and then figure out ways to actually go round behind and underneath it, so that it was no longer legal. That was the only way he liked to do things.

We had decided to take another trip to New Zealand, so in 1977 we caught a ship from Southampton to Auckland. Tom was so terrified of flying long distances at this stage (paranoid more like it) and for some extraordinary reason he decided we would make the trip on a Russian passenger ship. What he didn't realise when he made the booking was that being a communist ship, there was officially no 'first' or 'second' class. So, we ended up down in the bowels of this ship, the name of which I can't remember.

We flew from Barcelona up to London with the kids and caught the train down to Southampton docks. We boarded the ship and I was horrified to find our accommodation was below the waterline in a tiny little cabin with no portholes. Having recovered from this shock, I volunteered to go upstairs to book us in for the second dinner setting and was in a queue with hundreds of people doing the same thing.

I unwittingly found myself in behind a New Zealand couple, Andrew and Pauline, and during the course of the cruise we became very good friends. They were a lovely couple, but their charm increased exponentially when I discovered that they had a spacious cabin on the top deck, with a veranda outside, and the boys and I spent every day up there with them. Tom spent most days drinking in the public bar with the Russian Captain and his cronies.

I had to keep a 'bridle' on Nick for the whole voyage, as he was, as ever, so keen to dive over the side of the ship into the water. Our meals consisted of caviar every lunch and dinner, but the rest of the meal offerings were dreadful; Russian cuisine at its worst.

Our journey took us through the Panama Canal, which I found fascinating, particularly the more rudimentary parts where the canal walls consisted of glistening muck or clay, covered in myriad lizards and insects, and from which an intolerable stench emanated.

It all seemed very third world and strange to me. In saying that, the rest of the canal was amazing, particularly the artificial Gatun Lake, built 30 metres above sea level, which was created to reduce the amount of excavation work; a stroke of pure genius.

Having reached the Pacific end of the canal, one morning about three days out from Tahiti, the ship's ear-splitting siren started going off and we were told we were 'abandoning ship'. We dressed the boys in these huge, bulky lifejackets and I remember struggling up the steep, internal stairs with them to reach the lifeboats.

As we had been told to take only the absolute necessities, I grabbed our passports and my make-up bag and all my expensive jewellery. Before we clambered into the lifeboat, Tom, on the other hand, made his way to the dining room and gathered up a huge white tablecloth, into which he loaded bread rolls and bottles of brandy and some bottles of Coca Cola.

Believe me, we were the most popular people in the lifeboat. Apparently both the ship's generators were on fire, so we spent the better part of that day getting pissed in the lifeboats on brandy and coke. We were eventually allowed back on board later that night. Needless to say, Tom's fear of flying had been significantly assuaged by these sea-going experiences, and, after spending three weeks in the land of my birth, we flew back to Spain with no obvious repercussions.

Once back in Sitges I became reacquainted with my American friend Mac, who had been born on Beaver Island in Lake Michigan. I met Mac, or Leather Mac as he was called then, when I first arrived in Sitges, and we have remained good friends over all these past 55 years. Mac had one of the ubiquitous combi vans that all real travellers had to have, inside of which he had a small factory, making leather belts and bags which were very popular with the Sitges 'in crowd'. During his sojourn in Spain, Mac had met the gorgeous and very young Mardee, from Albany in up-state New York, who was attending university in Madrid, studying Spanish.

Mac eventually married Mardee and they came back to Sitges to start a new life together, and where she became a wonderful friend of mine and, after more than 50 years is still today my very best girlfriend.

They were around and about over all the years I was there, but as Mardee remarked recently, "You were very aloof", which was an understatement, especially regarding Tom. Even though he loved Mardee and had a lot of time for Mac, he wasn't the best at mixing with other people. Tom was the one who decided when and with whom he socialised. However, when we did see Mac and Mardee it was always so much fun.

In the winter we would plan a lunch up in the mountains with Mac and Mardee and the kids. Mardee and I would go to the local butcher shop in the morning with her big cane basket to buy 'chuletas de cordero' (lamb chops) and then on to the greengrocer for potatoes and vegetables. And then off we would all go, up into the hills where we had found a secluded spot, an old Civil War battleground by the looks of the burnt out houses there.

Mac always brought along the barbecue grill and we would send the boys off foraging for wood for the fire, while we took turns at going behind the bushes for a bit of 'slap and tickle'. I remember one day Mac had forgotten the grill, so, being Mac, he set about making one from all the war detritus in the area. From then on, that was our favourite grill.

Mardee insists I taught her to cook, which I can't remember at all, as we very rarely ate in. These days Mardee is a superb cook, way better than I will ever be, but she says she remembers me cooking amazing lunches of prawns Provençale and taking them to the antique shop – I have no recollection how, but that is her memory.

Mac's business had expanded exponentially over the years, and they now owned a large factory, right in the middle of town, with a number of Spanish people working for them. All I remember was they worked extremely hard, and this has served them well, as they now have an amazingly successful leather and linen business, *Estilo Emporio* (Spanish Emporium), based in Sydney, Australia, where they now live.

Another story Mardee tells is when we asked them to come over and look after the boys at the Casablanca, while we went to London for the weekend. Apparently, we were away for over a week, with no one knowing where we were – I don't remember this, needless to say.

Most mornings Mardee and I would go running together down to the Terramar Hotel (about three kilometres away from Sitges on the waterfront) and swim back. Other mornings we would take the boys to the station, to put them on the train to Castelldefels, then we would afterwards breakfast on beer and peanuts in the very basic old bar at the train station. The setting was nothing special but out friendship certainly was.

Mac tells an incredible story, where he says Tom asked him if he would like to go to Ireland with him, as he knew someone at Dublin airport who could help Mac sell his leather gear. This was definitely news to me; I think Tom just wanted someone to go with him for whatever reason. So, the two of them duly flew to Ireland, via London; again I have no idea why. It was certainly news to Mac as they checked into our favourite London pub, the Mayfair Hotel.

Mac phoned Mardee to tell her where he was, and she said, "Why don't you invite Chris for a drink? She's in London at the moment",

Chris being a girlfriend of hers. Chris duly arrived in the Mayfair bar and announced she was off to Paris on the train. Tom says, "Let me see your train ticket", and proceeded to tear it up and announced that he would buy her a plane ticket to Paris instead. This was just so typically Tom. Unfortunately, he didn't always follow through, and often left people in the 'lurch', as he lurched on his drunken way.

At this stage, disconcertingly, for Mac, Tom disappeared. This left Mac in the unenviable position of not only having to buy Chris an air ticket, but also to pay the Mayfair bill the next morning, which would not have been inconsiderable. He thought about just flying back to Spain, but eventually got hold of Tom's parents in Dublin, who said they believed Tom was there staying with them in Dublin.

So off he went to Dublin and finally caught up with Tom, who he found sitting on the floor of his family's living room in the dark, drinking whiskey out of the bottle with a couple of his brothers. Again, Tom disappears. He was on a major piss-up and could sometimes go three days and nights in this manner. He finally came home to his parents' house, and Mac again went and found him in a darkened room, in Mac's words, "sweatin blood" All the capillaries in Tom's face were exploding as he lay comatose for another two days. According to Mac, Tom then took off on his own, caught a small private plane to London and disappeared yet again.

At that stage Mac was then forced to return to Spain. How he still continued to be our friend after this experience is beyond me, as he wasn't exactly rolling in money at the time. He and Mardee have remained my good friends all our lives. However, he still describes Tom as having a "magnetic personality"

Mac owned a big old 'wild west' wagon that he asked if he could park at the Casablanca until he sold it. Unbelievably, someone set it on fire one night and nearly burnt our house down. Mac insists to this day that Tom did it.

On with our life. Our front living/dining room was jammed with antiques, paintings and the most beautiful rosewood dining table and chairs we had bought from Edwina. Edwina was a great old stick and I'm truly sorry I lost touch with her. She seemed to take a very dim view of my eventually leaving Tom, even under all the circumstances, which she may, or may not have been aware of. She should have though, as he once punched her off her stool at the bar, for some reason, known only to him.

I have recently been reading my diaries from these years, and page after page reads thus. *Woke up early to get the boys ready for school, walked them up to catch the train. Met Mardee for a beer in the station. Went for a run to the Terramar then back to join Tom in bed. Got up around 11 and showered etc then down to the Calipolis* (another hotel next door) *for a few G&Ts. Juan and his mate joined us, and the usual phone calls through to about 2.*

Met Fernando and Isobel in El Greco for lunch which went on all afternoon. I got home in time for Rosa to bring the boys back at 6 and I made them dinner and bathed them and got them into bed. Ann arrived to look after the kids. Went for drinks at El Mascaron with John and Henk. More phone calls. Went over to the Port to 'Mama's' for dinner at 9, and Edwina and Nerys joined us there. Late night drinks at Pachito, then the Capri. I came home early, left Tom there. Bed at midnight.

With many a change of personnel, every day was like this. In fact, when reading my diaries, it is like reading about someone else's life – I don't recognise most of the people who apparently made up our lives at the time.

Anybody could have told you that we all drank too much; in fact, we drank all day and every day, which goes some way to explaining why things started to go so pear-shaped. I don't want to dwell on the fact that Tom had been regularly giving me hidings, and more particularly, since we came to live at the Casablanca – only when he was drunk, but he broke my nose twice and my jaw once. I went to the local doctor each time, and each time he told me he was obliged to inform the police, which I had to beg him not to do. I can only say that would have made things way worse.

He was always terribly remorseful and would go off buying me diamond jewellery and whatever, but it didn't ever stop him from doing it again and again.

Unfortunately, the boys witnessed some of these very scary incidents when they were very little. It was hardly ever during an argument, but usually when I was fast asleep, and he would come home at three or four o'clock in the morning and wake me up by extinguishing his cigarette on some part of me and then proceed to punch and kick me.

There was one particular night which stands out in my mind, as it was so unbelievably demeaning and embarrassing. Tom had come home very late, very drunk, and yes, put out his cigarette on my bare bottom as I slept and proceeded to slap me and pull my hair, demanding I get up and come downstairs. Poor Nick heard the commotion and came in crying, hitting his father on the legs saying, "Leave Mummy alone".

He was unceremoniously kicked out of the way, and I was literally dragged down the stairs by my hair and out into the street where I was dumped in the gutter. Tom had come home with two Guardia Civil, who were standing smoking and looking on with amusement, I hate to say. I heard Tom say to them, 'Take this whore into Barcelona where she belongs, on the streets".

He then disappeared inside, and when I tried to go in, I found the door was locked and so was the kitchen door, so I was locked outside for the night stark naked, until somebody woke up in the morning to let me in. My diary the next day revealed, *I have never felt so sad and frightened.* Edwina commented, "You'll have to learn to leave a key hidden outside."

Mum and Dad came to Spain in 1979 for our 10th wedding anniversary – I have lovely photos of Dad standing beside Maria Teresa and our lawyer friend, Fernando, at the big party we threw at the Club de Mar. Someone had even thought of a cake (not me, as I didn't regard this as a celebration).

Tom had been in Barcelona on business all afternoon and arrived very drunk in the middle of the party. I have one photo of him looking at the cake and the next minute he is out on the terrace having a ciggie and falls over backwards into the Hobie Cats below, injuring his back.

Once again, we had to call the ambulance and off to St Pedro de Ribas Hospital he went. I didn't go with him that time as we had so many guests, and I wasn't really needed at the hospital. Some anniversary party.

While Mum and Dad were in Spain, we decided to go up to Madrid to visit Robby and Major Mike, who were now married, and where Mike was working for Rockwell International in Torrejon.

We took the train for once, instead of our usual taxi, and spent the entire seven-hour trip in the bar on the train – as we said, "sideways to Madrid". We drank the train bar out of gin and tonics. I had borrowed Isabel's full-length mink coat, to go with my full-length fox. Mum described this type of behaviour as "putting on the dog". Quite right too!

That was a marvellous time, probably the last good time Tom and I had together. He and Dad got on so well, and Dad really relaxed around Tom. They were both 'men's men', hard drinkers and gamblers, so I always knew they would get on.

Our CIA friend, Warren, lived in Madrid, and had booked us into a hotel over a whore bar, which resulted in our being woken up several times during the night. However, this never deterred Dad from his natural habit of waking up early, and the next morning he was up at his usual 6 am, cruising the corridors of the hotel with a bottle of champagne under his right armpit and a glass full in his left hand, and singing at the top of his voice, "Champagne Charlie is me name. Champagne drinking is me game!" I truly miss that man.

13. The Great Diamond Heist

He who rides the tiger is afraid to dismount.

– Winston Churchill

That was me, having a riotous old time riding the tiger, not realising it was fast becoming too late to dismount. You can't make up a story like this, so I will try to remember it as well as I can. Tom had been dealing in diamonds with a man in Barcelona, who will remain nameless, and a local fellow called Juan, in Sitges, whom Tom and I privately called 'The Pig' as he was fat and obnoxious, which is actually doing pigs a disservice. For Tom to negotiate these deals in a foreign country he needed a fully fashioned Spanish man as a partner, as we were merely 'Residentes'. Juan became our man for those reasons alone, as we weren't that keen on him as a person.

The deal was, Tom would receive a parcel of 'unsafe' emeralds, (in other words, emeralds that had been illegally thrown out of the mine) from his contact in Bogota, Columbia and would then exchange them for diamonds from the nameless man, and we would then proceed to try to sell the semi-legitimate diamonds. This actually worked like a charm for a while, and I was the recipient of some fabulous jewellery during these 'good times'. It was all highly illegal but there you go – that's probably what Tom liked most about it.

So, Tom was away in Geneva one weekend, negotiating some deal or other when I was woken by Juan's brother very early on the Saturday morning in Sitges. He had a fearful tale to tell (and fearful he well should have been, as it turned out). He told me that Juan had been driving to

Barcelona with our briefcase full of diamonds, emeralds, rubies, and sapphires, worth easily US$500,000 all up, when he apparently drove off the cliff and into the sea. (Incidentally, none of this jewellery had been paid for.)

I have to say, these kinds of road accidents happened all the time, as the road linking Sitges and Barcelona was extremely dangerous. However, this all sounded very suspicious, even to me. I phoned Tom at his hotel in Geneva and gave him the gist of the story and told him that Juan was up in the hospital in Saint Pedro de Ribas with severe grazing but was alive. Tom's first question was, "Where is the briefcase?" Of course.

I had been told that the briefcase had gone down with the car and that Juan was lucky to still be alive. Tom instructed me to go up to the hospital and get a nurse to take a swab of his skin to see if Juan had actually been in the salt water. Of course, I couldn't do anything of the sort, but I did go to see him, and he looked appropriately all cut up and grazed. (As it turned out later, his rather brutal compatriot thieves had rolled him in the gravel, before sending his car – incidentally a very fine Mercedes – off over the cliff; however, this wasn't the story they were feeding me).

Tom did not believe their story for one second and he was desperate to get back to Sitges to get to the bottom of yet another drama. He tried booking himself on a flight, but they were all full, then he tried to get a private plane, but his Irish accent put paid to that (1970s, the time of the Troubles in Ireland.) So, he hailed a taxi in downtown Geneva and asked the very startled Swiss driver to drive him to Sitges in Spain. As he left the city of Geneva, he stopped off to buy a bottle of Cognac and settled in for the long and expensive trip.

In the meantime, Juan and his co-conspirators, made up of several town police, and other town officials, including the Mayor, thought they had pulled off the 'crime of the century' and were busy dividing up the loot. The wrath of God was about to descend upon them in the guise of one very pissed-off Tom Corley.

He arrived back home 24 hours after leaving Switzerland, having driven all day and all night. As soon as he got home, he went off and bought the taxi driver a new set of clothes and toilet gear. This guy stayed with us for a couple of weeks, driving us around in his black BMW with blacked out windows – perfect for the 'cloak and dagger' stuff we then became involved in. God only knows what his wife thought of these goings on in Spain, and his not coming back to Switzerland. He seemed happy enough in his new guise.

Tom and I decamped to our favourite retreat on the coast, the Hotel Los Pinos (The Pines), where we set up shop, and he was then ready to get to the bottom of this sudden and, you could say, unfortunate turn of events. He demanded that Juan come to the hotel and tell us exactly what had happened. That fat man was sweating so much I thought he would have a heart attack. After a few hours of Tom grilling, him he broke down and confessed that it was all a big con and promised to get all the loot back. This turned out to be much harder than we initially thought.

Apparently, there had been about 10 of these maladroits, joining Juan's merry band of thieving bastards, all thrilled with themselves to be in on such a dastardly plot. I guess here I could make the wry observation in hindsight, how did we think we were any better, engaging in an illicit diamond trade?

Although Juan had taken the lion's share for himself, the other people involved had variously given some of their stash away, swapped it, and some had even lost it (yeah, right). Naturally, they had absolutely no idea what to do with precious stones, and to try to speculate as to why Juan had invested his now dodgy looking future in these true innocents left me speechless.

Looking back after all this time, I would consider the idea that someone was possibly putting the 'hard word on' Juan, having heard a whisper about what he was up to with Tom. As they didn't fancy taking Tom on, they had decided to put the screws on Juan to include them in a heist. It would make a great movie, if it wasn't so silly, and at the same time so serious for all of us.

When you are dealing in precious stones, they all come wrapped in a special waxy paper, and these people just didn't have a clue. However, one by one, they were eventually inveigled to come to the Los Pinos with their pathetic bundles of loot, and shamefacedly handed most of it back. It certainly led me to realise that these guys were a lot more fearful of Tom than I ever could have imagined.

We moved from the coast to the penthouse in the Ritz Hotel in Barcelona, for some reason via a race to the Barcelona airport where I was meant to look as though I was leaving on a plane. I have no idea why. I had diamonds stashed in the bottom of my Louis Vuitton make-up bag. By this time our life had become so crazy I was going along with anything and everything, so to start questioning Tom at this stage would have been very difficult.

We settled into the Ritz with our unnamed diamond man, who brought his weighing scales and waxy paper to the hotel to start putting everything back together again. This took well over a week, of us going through each person's stash, stone by stone, with me sitting cross-legged on the lush carpet in our suite, helping as best I could.

It was around about this time that we became aware that there was an awful lot of the stones missing. This was a total disaster, as the 'Man from Bogota' was due in the next few weeks and he would want to be paid, somewhere in the region of US$250,000. We were in real trouble, which was now only just beginning for us.

With this huge deficit looming over our heads, Tom decided we would fly down to Marbella and hole up in the Melia don Pepe, the fanciest hotel down there. During all this time I was relying on my wonderful babysitters and nannies to look after the boys – I had no choice.

This hotel was, in those days, full of rich Arabs, and Tom was soon walking around in full Arab kit, with his cowboy boots on underneath his long, white robe. Don't even ask me what I was doing all this time, but I do recall we had an awful row in our hotel room one night, and Tom did one of his disappearing acts for 24 hours. Regrettably, this would have been just one more awful row over nothing.

During the next few days, Tom managed to sell over US$150,000 worth of gems on to these happy Middle Eastern customers, and we arrived back in Sitges thinking we could possibly get out of this mess unscathed.

Juan we dismissed as useless, but Tom was surprisingly lenient with him, probably coming to the realisation that if he wanted to continue with this dodgy business, he definitely had a dodgy partner to help him.

The Bogota man was due any day to collect his money, and we were still around US$100,000 short, so Tom then did something extremely stupid. He was offered a packet of diamonds for sale at US$25,000, and he then found someone who would pay US$75,000 for them. I've always believed, that if something sounds too good to be true, it usually is. Also, he was buying these diamonds sight unseen – an unwise decision at any time, but a really amateur and, as it turned out, a desperate decision for someone like Tom.

These diamonds duly arrived and when I set eyes on this latest 'acquisition' I could see that all the jewellery had PRICE TAGS on them. "Tom, these have to be stolen goods", and of course they were. If we thought we had problems before; now our real troubles were just beginning.

However, as Juan had already arranged the deal, he went ahead and sold them on to the person concerned, and we seemed at first glance to have 'got away with it'. So unwise. In Spain in the 70s you very rarely got away with a robbery. I'm not sure as to how they traced the crime back to Tom, but that's how his shady purchase came back to burn us.

We were sitting out in the bar of the Casablanca a couple of days later, actually 21 March, 1980, the day after my 33rd birthday. Two really scruffy young guys came in and asked the barman for Señor Tomas Corley. Immediately Tom guessed they were the secret police and said to me, "I'm off to the 'free hotel', go and get my passport".

Just out of interest, I always wondered how Tom ever made it through Customs or on to a plane with his vandalised Irish passports. They always had pages ripped out of them, lists of phone numbers in the back, names of friends and accomplices, pictures he drew of people– you name it – writing all over the pages. All his passports were similarly totally defaced.

Sure enough, once Tom had his passport, they hustled him away in the Black Maria. I waited the entire day and night to hear from him and in the end, after phoning Fernando, our lawyer friend in Sitges, I went to see him in his house there. He said he could do nothing to help Tom. However, he gave me the name of a very expensive solicitor in Barcelona, and the next day I drove in for a meeting with a lawyer we shall call Javier.

We met in his home, a beautiful old house in the city and I handed over something equivalent to £5,000 and he went off to see what he could find out. I went home, and Javier phoned me a few hours later, and had found Tom, now in the *Modelo*, a huge prison, built for 1,000 prisoners. However, there were nearly 3,000 inmates ensconced there when Tom arrived in handcuffs.

According to Tom he instructed Javier to, "Get me out of this fucking shithole ASAP". I don't know about that, but I do know that any form of incarceration in Spain at that time was something to be avoided at all costs. I know Tom thought he was bullet-proof, and he was a hard man to stop when he had a gleam in his eye and a shonky idea, but even for him being in jail was a step up in new experiences.

Diary Entry for Day 17 of Tom's Incarceration

Woke up very early, without much sleep. I had a very strange dream about Tom in the sea with four other men and it was a jail, with one man teaching them to hold their breath under water. Then we got him out and he and I were fighting and fighting.

I never thought I could keep on living like this – I am living in a dream until Tom comes out. Tuesday seems like a million miles away. I am living each day like an automaton, not even knowing what I do. I clean like mad every morning to get my mind off where Tom is. I found myself screaming at the children that I was going to leave them. How awful. We painted eggs and had an Easter egg hunt and I gave the kids some chocolate eggs. Chris came and I made roast chicken for lunch. (Chris was the father of one of Alan's friends).

When I finally got to visit Tom with Javier, during a lawyer's visit we had nearly two hours of privacy, where he related to me at length his experiences up to that point. He had to share a two-person cell with four other guys. They all took turns at sleeping and one of the gay guys did Tom's laundry for him. He was extremely fastidious so it must have been torture for him to be in there for that reason alone. Another inmate did the food shopping in the jail market. Tom washed the cos lettuce for the salad every day in the toilet's basin. This was a man totally devoted to eating in only the best restaurants and who had never, ever been in our kitchen, except to get another bottle of wine from the fridge.

Tom told me about watching a guy being knifed to death in the 'beer queue'. Prisoners weren't fed but they could line up for a free beer every day. All the wives and mothers had to queue outside the jail every morning to bring in the food for their men. Tom got himself a job checking all the food as it came in, making sure there were no saws or guns I suppose. He had to poke the cooked chickens and oranges with a knitting needle – the weird things you remember! The drugs came over the top of the jail walls and anyone with money could order their dinner from a very expensive restaurant outside the prison walls, or a whore from the nearest cat house.

Tom talked to a German guy who had been there for over ten years and who still didn't know what he was in there for – he didn't have a cent to his name, so couldn't afford to hire a lawyer to get him out. Our lawyer was bleeding me dry but he was getting there slowly. Getting to see Tom became a very fraught and extremely stressful exercise, as I wasn't prepared to join the hundreds of women who lined up outside the jail from early in the morning.

The queues were hours' long, and I involved myself in this rigmarole just the one time. As if things weren't bad enough, I had just come out of hospital from an operation for a torn cartilage on my left meniscus, which left me in plaster for several weeks. This had me hobbling along on crutches, and being jostled by very loud and pushy ladies in the hot sun. I counted myself lucky that, unlike them, I wasn't burdened with baskets of food and drinks.

When I finally got up to the visiting room, I was ushered into a corridor with a long line of cells and was escorted towards a chair outside Tom's cell. It was beyond awful. I picked up the phone and tried to talk to Tom, but with all the other ladies screaming into phones just meters away from me, I couldn't hear a thing he was saying. Also, it didn't help that he was in a foul mood and was asking me questions I didn't know the answers to anyway. All in all, a hideous exercise all round. I vowed to never go through that again, while at the same time having so much compassion for all these hundreds of women for whom lining up day after day was their only option.

Diary Entry For Day 35 of Tom's Incarceration

Spent all morning cleaning and making the house all ready for Tom – it looks lovely. Made a big fruit salad and had some for lunch. Spent the rest of the afternoon waiting, pacing up and down, and then Javier called and I took the train to Barcelona and waited in the bar for him. Finally, at 6 o'clock Javier and I went to see Tom. He looked so good. Talking all business, and shockingly has already set up a deal with some Irishman in prison. Oh, help.

Diary Entry For Day 91 of Tom's Incarceration

Very hot long day. Waiting and waiting all day to hear from Javier about what the Judge said. Really, truly awful. Prue and I were in the station at 8 to put the kids on the train – poor Alan I couldn't go to his prize-giving day, and he got a prize for Special English – whatever that is. (Terry's wife Prue had come down from Ireland to stay with me, and she was a huge help). *All our waiting for nothing once again – Javier rang to say he couldn't get the Judge. Sometimes I hate him!*

Poor Javier, I was pretty hard on him. From the start, he had been arranging for me to go with him to the lawyer's part of the jail, where Tom and I could at least have a conversation, but were not allowed any physical contact. No doubt these visits were achieved by the bribing of whichever guards were on duty at the time, and this cost was no doubt being added to my rapidly escalating bills which were arriving on a regular basis from Javier.

I hadn't told anyone in Sitges that Tom was in jail, except for Dani and Rosamaria. These were two gay friends we had recently met, and who Tom had made part of his cadre, as Dani knew her way around the Spanish legal system and was a very smart cookie. She had been a child during the Civil War and had some unbelievable stories of those times, such as swimming out from the beach at Sitges to pick up bits of oranges thrown overboard from passing ships, as she was without food and starving. Rosamaria was a nurse who worked up at the hospital in San Pedro de Ribas.

Just a quick story here whereupon I saved a man's life. Rosamaria knew my blood type, from when I had had my knee operation at her hospital, so she phoned us one day when the call went out on the radio for someone, anyone, who had B Positive blood – apparently a blood type that was very rare in Cataluña. An ambulance was sent to collect me, and I sat and gave what looked to me like huge amounts of blood to a man who had suffered a fall into an empty swimming-pool, and so you could say, I saved his life! Needless to say, no cup of tea and a gingernut for me. A big glass of brandy was put into my 'weak and shaking' hands!

Dani had taken part in several of the meetings leading up to the robbery of the jewellery store that resulted in Tom's arrest, and she was also sent to jail to a women's prison (where she was raped). She got out after a few weeks as she was small fry in the whole event. I also hadn't told my family or Tom's about his arrest and imprisonment at that stage. In fact, I hadn't told anyone but Prue. It just seemed all so awful and unbelievable, and I was dealing with the enormity of it one day at a time.

Creditors were pounding on the door of the Casablanca, and so too were those other types of unsavoury characters who loved to hang around when they thought something bad might have happened to you. How people love to see that 'the mighty have fallen'. I moved with the children into Dani and Rosamaria's huge home in the Vinyet, an area outside of town, with houses built by Cuban exiles in the '60s.

Quite soon after moving in with these wonderful women, I met their other 'lodger', an Argentinian doctor, Daniel, who was working at the hospital in Barcelona as an anaesthetist. He was a few years' younger than me, but we hit it off immediately, and I have to say I was quite taken with him, as he was a very good looking boy.

Over the next few weeks we all shared some very convivial lunches in the garden, with Rosamaria and I preparing the escalivada, or Catalan roasted vegetables, including eggplant, red peppers, onions and tomatoes, and with Daniel 'manning' the barbecue, and pouring the beers, and Dani trying desperately to corral my boisterous sons. It was so good for me to be around happy, normal people, as opposed to what had become *my normal,* of creditors and lawyers, and an increasingly angry and paranoid Tom.

Daniel also got on really well with my boys, and we had some fun afternoons, taking them after school to the local 'parque de atracciones' playground) and later to a local bar with a slot machine, which I had never let them play on before. It was so freeing to just relax in a normal way, with lots of laughter and teasing. I really needed this time off from worrying and stressing out, and inevitably, our friendship led to a more intimate relationship.

At first, I felt terribly guilty about this, but Dani and Rosamaria seemed more than happy with us, and I realised at this stage that my relationship with Tom had become so volatile and so violent, there was no joy in it any more, even though I knew I still loved him.

To be honest, I didn't really try to keep our friendship a secret from any of my friends, who were, like Dani and Rosamaria, quite simply thrilled for me. I started smiling again, laughing and joking again and even my physical health improved, as I had lost a lot of weight over the past few months. Life just seemed to be happier around Daniel.

I suspect someone from Sitges had written to Tom in jail, and informed him of this latest development, and although I denied it to the end, it made him, understandably, even more paranoid and angry. I guess you could say I was 'playing with fire' in the most dangerous manner.

That relationship obviously came to a halt when Tom got out of jail, but Daniel came to visit me in New Zealand when I first got back there. However, I really wasn't ready for another relationship of any kind, at that time, and he returned to Barcelona and I have always stayed in touch with him, visiting him in Bariloche when he went back to live in Argentina.

So, in the meantime, I continued on living with Dani and Rosamaria, as I felt relatively safe there, and I had very trusted instant babysitters when I needed to move fast, such as when I found out that the man from Bogota had finally arrived in Sitges: and he meant business.

I arranged to meet him over in a bar in Porto Aiguadolç and of course he wanted to know where his money was, and when I told him Tom was in jail, he mentioned that it would be even easier to kill him in there! He had the most piercing blue eyes – similar to Tom's 'machine-gun' eyes, and he was a very scary person indeed.

Obviously, the man from Bogota would rather have the money than kill Tom, so Tom and I worked out some deal with him – I can't actually remember how, but Juan must have had some of the money left from the jewellery shop robbery. Our finances were in a terrible mess, and since Tom had gone to jail the police had closed down the antique shop and put big locks and chains on the door.

We were allowed to keep the Casablanca as that was our home, but even the Bar Capri had to be sold and the money went as reimbursement to the Spanish State for having to keep Tom in jail. That's how it worked in Spain in those days.

14. Tom Out of Jail and the End of our Marriage

Three months, actually 98 days, later, on the 26th of June, 1980 our lawyer, Javier, finally secured a hearing in the Palacio de Justicia, the courthouse in the town where the robbery had taken place, Villa Franca, further up the highway from St Pedro de Ribas. Javier drove me up there, and we watched as Tom arrived on a bus, handcuffed to two other prisoners – a real fair dinkum criminal.

Tom told me to go to the nearest Bodega to buy a case of beer, which I did, and which made me very popular with the cops and crims alike. So we sat there enjoying cold, crisp bottles of San Miguel, the beer of the region, while waiting for the judge to appear.

We had been warned that the judge may need to be bribed, if things didn't go the way we had been led to be believe by Javier. So when he finally handed down a sentence of two years, to be spent in a huge prison several hundred miles away inland, we realised that yes, we were going to have to offer him a bribe.

There was certainly no way that Tom was going back to jail, so I was forced to borrow the rather alarming amount from Javier, and in that supremely unconventional way, secured Tom's freedom. I then spent the next couple of weeks scavenging, and borrowing from friends to pay Javier back. It turns out that bribing a judge wasn't an entirely unprecedented state of affairs.

All up, this whole totally unnecessary episode probably cost us well over £50,000. It was just as well we had had a decent amount of cash in the bank from all Tom's 'wheeling and dealing'. However, these funds were now severely depleted. Unfortunately, Tom had now become so paranoid after his experiences in jail, he started to accuse me of stealing all the money. He wouldn't accept that the vast majority of it had gone to Javier and to the judge. It wasn't appreciated when I pointed out it was all due to Tom and Juan's stupid mistake of facilitating a robbery.

I finally lost all patience with him for even suggesting I had stolen any money, and his burgeoning anger at the world in general, turned into a senseless rage at me, in particular. Our lives were starting to unravel, and I could sense that things would never be the same again.

Diary entry 20th July 1980.
Feeling very nice tonight, even if things are not going so well – at least Tom and I are fine.

I kept fooling myself that everything was fine, when it clearly wasn't. I can see from more diary entries that we were busy having sex at all hours of the day and night, and so on I went, trying to make it all work.

It is 45 years since I left Tom, and since I left my life and everything I knew and loved. Because the ending was such an incredibly stressful time, there are whole chunks of it that I simply can't remember, or have deliberately expunged from my memory what I was feeling at the time. This is why I have resorted to reading my 1980 diary, to help me remember what it all felt like.

However, doing this has been an incredibly depressing exercise, as my whole life had been turned upside down. Trying to keep something like Tom's imprisonment secret in a small town was obviously impossible, and I have one rather sad page in the diary of those people I could trust and those I couldn't. A list of 'good people' and one of 'bad people' and I hesitate to add, the bad people list was longer.

During the whole time Tom was in jail I felt terribly alone, and a sort of siege mentality had set in, as I shuttled in and out of Barcelona, sometimes twice a day, seeing the lawyer, seeing Spanish people we had been doing business with, some wanting money, some owing us money. In some ways I was incredibly busy which was good because it took my mind off the terrible situation we were in, but I was exhausted all the time, juggling looking after the boys, and racing off to Barcelona at the drop of a hat, all at the slightest possibility I could get to see Tom.

According to my diary, and I still find this quite intriguing, I used to get so excited about the possibility of going to see Tom and would spend hours waiting in the lawyer's home in the city, for him to either take me to the jail, or give me the bad news, and I would have to get the train back to Sitges. One phrase really sticks in my mind regarding these very fraught, sometimes impromptu visits, was my happy report to the diary at night: *He looked wonderful.*

I can't imagine that he did, but I was always just so happy and excited to see him. Also, according to my diary entries at the time, at this stage I was sure I was dealing with someone who wasn't well. Apart from the alcoholism and violence, his mood changes were terrifying.

Now that Tom was no longer in prison, as if the previous months hadn't been crazy enough, he now started to go missing for days at a time, only coming home to sleep, and I was living on the edge from day to day. Often, he didn't come home at all, making me so anxious as to his whereabouts and what he was up to.

He became very secretive about his business dealings, and almost seemed to blame me for the fact that he had ended up in jail. To be honest, I had never really known much about what he was up to, but as his wife, I had gone along with it through the good times and the bad.

I finally began to realise that our way of life was not a healthy one for our boys as they grew older, and I knew that it was now up to me to change that. However, in his present strange mood, I realised that Tom was not about to have a conversation in that direction. It is extremely painful to read the last few months in my diary of that year 1980, as our relationship had totally broken down.

Looking back, it is hard to believe that from such a wonderful beginning, our lives had come to this point. I was becoming certain that Tom would never let me leave, and that he could very well kill me. Because we were fighting so much, and I was very afraid of him, I suggested that the boys and I went to live in Warren's apartment on the waterfront, which meant that Tom could see his children every day. As he had never shown any interest in seeing them before, I realised this was just me grasping at straws. I desperately wanted to leave, but I knew I couldn't. For a start, I had no money stashed away and we continued to live day to day as we always had.

When he wasn't away for days at a time, he wanted me with him day and night for some reason. As I couldn't keep up with his crazy hours, this resulted as always in his coming home at 4 o'clock most mornings and waking me up for an argument about something, anything. Strangely, he never once asked me about Daniel, or referred to anything of that sort. Maybe he was too proud.

One of the last beatings he gave me involved a huge terracotta flowerpot, which he found on our bedroom balcony, and with which he proceeded to smash over my head. I truly feared for my life that night, and I hate to admit that I was screaming and crying and making a terrible noise to try to wake anyone else up, as I was so afraid that Tom would kill me.

Of course there was nobody there except my poor boys, and the looks on their faces as they stood in the doorway still haunts me. The sad part is they were basically afraid of the stranger beating their mother, as Tom had so little to do with them by that time.

The week before that incident he had raped me in Araceli's bed. I had taken to sleeping in her small room downstairs by the kitchen, when she was away, and he found me there one night, as he roared around the house looking for me. Naturally, he assumed that I didn't want to sleep with him, so with some muttering about his 'conjugal rights' he smashed a glass by my bed and proceeded to hold the broken shard over my face as he raped me. "I'll cut your face up to make sure no one ever looks at you again."

This time I was too afraid to scream, but Alan had heard the noise from upstairs and came running down to find his father sitting on top of me. He ordered Alan to go get his pistol, which he kept by his bed upstairs. Luckily for all of us, this terrible incident went no further. Such terrible, scary times couldn't continue.

Tom never saw his Irish passport again, as the State had requisitioned it, so when he got out of jail, he somehow managed to get himself a diplomatic passport which I remember was red. I have no idea how he managed to do that, but it was no doubt through one of the extremely dodgy characters he had met in jail, and whose names and numbers he had inked down his arm when he was in there.

The boys and I went back to living with Dani and Rosamaria, when he decided to go off to New York, As usual, I was not let in on any details as to why he wanted to go there, but it signalled the chance of a few days to try to calm down and lead a normal life for me and the boys. If Tom seemed so determined to continue with his dodgy lifestyle, I was beginning to wonder if the children and I could continue to live it with him.

One night while he was away he phoned me drunk from New York and told me that he had two men waiting outside the house to break my legs, warning me not to go "out of the town". It was such a bizarre way of threatening me, but for some reason, after 12 years of intermittent abuse, something in me just cracked – I guess it's called the 'straw that broke the camel's back'. Right then and there I made the decision that I could not go on living like this, in fear of my life, and so desperately unhappy. I decided I had to leave.

That night the boys and I took a taxi to Barcelona and caught a midnight flight to Madrid on one of the hourly flights between Barcelona and Madrid, that took place day and night. Robby and Mike were now living in Madrid, so I took a taxi to their apartment, and from there I phoned Mum and Dad and told them I had to come home. Dad didn't ask any questions, and said he would call me back. True to his word, he phoned me back after two hours to tell me his travel agent would arrange for three airline tickets to be sent to the Swiss Air booking office in Madrid. It was almost as though he knew what had been happening, even though I still hadn't told them Tom had been in jail.

I left the boys with Robby and Mike and flew back to Sitges, hoping against hope I could pack our things before Tom got back from New York. No such luck, and when he arrived back I said I needed to talk to him. With great trepidation I told him I was leaving him, and that the boys and I were going home to New Zealand. I made sure that this conversation took place in front of Steve and Pepe in the bar, as I was terrified of what his reaction would be, but he just went deathly silent, and stared and stared at me which was very unnerving. I think he couldn't quite believe what I was saying, but he knew better than to touch me in front of the guys.

True to form, he never once asked about the boys, and was more concerned about what I would say to Dad. However, he seemed so stunned by this new turn of events he left me alone and went off drinking with his mates.

Having packed two suitcases for me and the boys with our clothes and some toys, I had the crazy notion that I might be able to take some of the paintings I had collected over the years, and I also packed all the rest of the children's toys and clothes, and precious articles such as photograph albums and my winter clothes (furs of course!). I arranged for a shipping firm from Barcelona to come and collect this modest amount of belongings I considered to be mine, and although they picked them up, Tom steadfastly refused to pay for the shipping container. There it remained in the depot in Barcelona, until I was eventually informed, they had auctioned off the paintings and burned the rest. That is something I had to try not to think about too much – all my photos.

This was an extremely traumatic time and a lot of it is a complete blur, with most of the pages in my diary at that time being completely empty. I flew back up to Madrid and stayed with Robby and Mike until our flight to New Zealand. I couldn't believe that my once wonderful life had come to such a sad and terrible ending.

Please believe me, I was always very aware that the life we led was slightly off the planet, but I never stopped to think that it probably wasn't actually sustainable, as it was all so exciting and so much fun at the time. This is probably a good time in this narrative to try to explain how and why Tom was such a charismatic character.

For a start, he was a physically imposing person, 6 ft tall and with a magnetic demeanour, and with piercing blue eyes, described by a former friend of his in London as 'machine-gun eyes' which could be quite disconcerting when directed your way.

Strangely enough, he could be quite distant with people he couldn't be bothered with, which was nearly everyone who wasn't involved in the 'cadre' with which he surrounded himself. Except for barmen and waiters. He was always unfailingly interested in, and friendly to anyone serving him, and was always very generous with his tips. This meant that everywhere we went we were treated like VIPs, and always got good service.

Even when I first met him, I was astounded at his loyal followers. It was almost a cult, and he fostered that idea, with everyone outside his orbit always wanting to be in it. These cult members could be dropped without warning as someone more interesting or more useful came along. There was no question that at any time Tom wasn't in charge. He could hold the floor for hours at a time with his stories, and his philosophising on life.

Since I returned to New Zealand, I have met many people who knew him over the years, in London, Spain and in Australia, and they all have their own story to tell, sometimes in awe, of their experiences with him. To this day I remain in awe of him, keeping in mind he was ten years' older than me, and I loved him right to the end. In my diary I am still in love with him, even when I had to leave him. I read somewhere once the words, 'the skill at power games, the attractiveness, the elegance, the charming menace', which describe him perfectly.

So, why didn't I leave earlier? As you can tell, to begin with I was dazzled and blinded by him, and he continually told me, 'I don't just love you, I adore you'. Heady stuff. I have a postcard he sent to my sister Robby during one of the many times when Tom and I were staying in London, which simply read, "Escargot Bourguignonne, Lobster Thermidor, Château Mouton Rothschild '57 and Penny. See you soon, Tom."

However, as the violence continued, it was hard to reconcile with his loving words. He only ever hit me when he was drunk (which was obviously a lot of the time), and was always incredibly remorseful the next day, showering me with diamonds and furs. I can sense the reader roling their eyes here.

The drinking definitely became worse, to the point that he was very rarely sober, and by the time I left him he was in real trouble. The months leading up to his arrest and afterwards were a nightmare, as he would disappear for days at a time and come home in such a terrible state he would take to his bed for days, as sick as a dog. This was happening on a regular basis, and Tom was drinking all night, sleeping all day and then disappearing again.

I recall one night he came staggering back at 3 o'clock in the morning after a long session at the Hotel Calipolis next door, and was attacked just outside my bedroom window at the Casablanca. I could hear him shouting and swearing as this person tried to rob him, and I truly hoped they would kill him. That's how bad it had become.

I have talked long and searchingly with my boys, particularly as they get older, and they have told me they were deeply affected by the violence of those years, and also by the fact that Tom was basically an absent father. However, when they were older, and visited him over the following years, he always told them I had been the love of his life, and he certainly loved them as he got to know them better. I am so proud of the wonderful men they have turned out to be, loving husbands and terrific fathers, with no hint of their father's darker side.

I didn't go back to Sitges again, until 1986, but I made sure the boys went to visit Tom every year. After the boys and I left, Tom moved down to the Canary Islands, possibly because there were so many people he owed money to in Sitges. I don't really know why he moved way down there, but he ended up marrying Maggie, his secretary who was 15 years younger than him, and they lived in the Canary Islands and then Marbella. Then she divorced him, and he eventually married Jerry in Phuket who was even younger. The boys both went over to visit him there, and were with him up to a couple of weeks before he died. Tom died of cancer in Thailand in 2007 at the age of 69, having been a drinker and a smoker all his life.

I was determined, once I was back in New Zealand, that I would not dwell on the last few months of my life with Tom, as they were so desperately sad, I could easily have found myself in a really bad mental state. So, instead, I have always tried to remember all the good times, and there were so many of them, so that my memories of Tom are good memories. I figured I would do nobody any good by dwelling on the terrible ending, so I just picked myself up, and 'got on with it'.

15. Epilogue

I have obviously (so far) lived to tell the tale, happily and safely in New Zealand. I have to say, when I first arrived here in 1980, New Zealand was nothing like it is now – there were very few New Zealand wines, no decent coffee, very few good restaurants, and I felt like a fish out of water. It was as though I had landed on Mars.

However, I have since come to appreciate what a truly beautiful country I was born in, with so many innovative and interesting people, who I obviously was too busy to be interested in before I left! I'm so glad I came home, even though I do miss Spain, especially the wonderful people there, the food, and their particularly attractive (to me) way of life.

When the boys and I arrived at Auckland airport all those years' ago, Dad was there to meet us, and took us back to the farm at Waiau Pa, south of Auckland, and there was my Mum, and my wonderful godfather, Dave waiting for us. We opened a bottle of Cordoniū the Spanish traditional sparkling wine that had been such a big part of our lives in Sitges, and was one of Dad's favourites. The vineyard which was founded in 1551, was situated just up the road from where we lived in Spain.

Mum whisked the boys away, making them dinner and getting them ready for bed, while I sat with my now two favourite men in the world, who insisted that I 'tell them everything'. That was very hard, as you can imagine, as I had bottled it all up for so long, and I found it very difficult to talk to them about the abuse, and about all the other dramas that had made up my life recently. My beautiful godfather was in tears

– this man a veteran of the Second World War with Dad.

They had both known Tom, and Dad in particular, was good friends with him, at least in the area of gambling and horse-racing: I doubt that they ever discussed Tom's 'wheeling and dealing' during those times, or any of the other shenanigans he used to get up to.

It felt good for me to finally be telling the truth to my Dad, and I told him about my brief relationship with Daniel. Dad confided that Tom had phoned him while I was in the air on my trip home and had told him to be very wary of me as I was on drugs. I can only regard this as a last ditcch effort from a desperate man, who now realised he had lost everything that he had valued in his life – it was just way too late. It also possibly exposed to just what depths Tom had sunk, by telling a father his daughter was on drugs, especially as it was totally untrue. It was a huge betrayal of their former friendship, and incidentally, of our relationship.

Just a note here to put the ledger straight, during all our drunken partying and crazy lifestyle, neither Tom nor I ever did drugs; we just weren't interested. I didn't even attempt to defend myself against such a spurious charge, as it must have been obvious to Dad as soon as he met me that I was still just Pen, who liked a drink with the rest of them.

The boys and I lived with my parents for three months out on the farm, and Mum and Dad were just so supportive and loving, while I tried to work out what to do with my shattered life, and more importantly, how I could get the boys back into school and into life in New Zealand. At this stage Dad realised I would need a car and arranged to buy one through an old friend of mine, who was a car dealer and a big fan of my Dad, and he drove my 'new' car out to the farm for us.

Now I was mobile, so my lovely third sister, Judi and her husband Greg insisted that I move into town to live with them in their home on the North Shore of Auckland, so that we could enrol Alan in school there, and look for a kindergarten for Nick. Also, I needed to start making money as I had basically left Spain with nothing but the clothes on our backs. Judi and Greg had a young family, the same age as my boys so they all went off to school and kindergarten together every day. It was bliss for me to be in such a loving, normal family, and it allowed me to get stuck into looking for work, which to be fair, I hadn't really had to worry about for the last 12 years.

That being said, I had never been one to shy away from work as a young person, so I advertised in the local paper as a house-cleaner at $5 an hour, and very soon had enough paying clients every day to support myself and my boys. My old friend Lulu, now married to Philip and living back in New Zealand, found me a great big old house near where they lived in Ponsonby, so I could be closer to travel to all my clients. I managed to enrol both the boys in the Ponsonby Primary school, and we moved over there to the 'moon and stars' house as the boys called it, as the ceiling in my bedroom was painted as a night sky.

With all the wonderful support I received in those first couple of years, from everyone in my family and from random friends I had all but forgotten about, we three, or The Three Musketeers as we called ourselves, just went from strength to strength. The boys, shockingly immediately completely lost all their Spanish language, never to be recovered, and started to speak English with a terrible Kiwi accent, so that they could blend in, as all kids want to do.

I met my second husband, Michael, in 1982 at a dinner party, a set-up by friends; he was a very unusual, eccentric and supremely interesting man. A surfer, a diver, a Shakespeare mastermind, and a devotee of Mozart and Beethoven, and a terrific cook and raconteur – what more could I ask for? Me and my 'interesting' men!

He had some amazing friends around the world, some of whom, unsurprisingly, knew Tom Corley, and we have spent a lot of time travelling and visiting them all.

The boys grew up, both of them fine athletes and in their own way, scholars, and went on to become the wonderful husbands and fathers they are today. Even so, I am always very aware of the fact that the trauma they experienced in Spain left its mark on them. I feel that we all missed out, with the man that I married never really exhibiting any interest in being a real father to his sons when they were little, and when they most needed it.

That is for me to acknowledge, and I will always live with that fact. I probably didn't worry about it at the time in Spain, as I could see how happy they were with their friends and at school, and we occasionally had some wonderful times with Tom, up in the mountains and at the Club de Mar with friends and family. And, of course, all those trips to New Zealand to see their grandparents.

Michael and I bought a property out on Great Barrier Island where we ran a luxury lodge and restaurant, planting a vineyard and making our own wine. Sadly, I left Mickey (as I always called him) out there in 2007. It was so awful, as we had been great mates and were so well suited. I never wanted to leave my island paradise, but we were both very unhappy, for various reasons, and someone had to go – and that someone had to be me.

I moved to gorgeous Waiheke Island, as my sister Anna was living there, and moved in with my brother-in-law Shane. Now, this probably sounds just all wrong, but Shane had been a wonderful friend for years, and was divorced from my little sister, Heather, and it was a totally platonic relationship – let's just get that straight. Anna and I did a lot of travelling during that time, to the Greek Islands and Italy, Africa and Spain, and I also made some wonderful friends out on that island too.

In 2016 I moved to the beautiful little surf town of Raglan on the West coast of the North Island of New Zealand, where I bought a dreamy tiny home looking out over the water. Being a little too old for surfing now, I have a stand-up paddle board and take my lovely rescue dog, Wade, out on the harbour with me. New, wonderful friends and neighbours now make up my busy life, and of course my fabulous four grand-children who make me happy just looking at them. I am loving every minute of it.

Meeting 'the man in black in that summer of 69' is still the most important and most exciting episode in my life, and that will never change. Meeting Tom was the real beginning of my life, and in a very short time he had become the most important part of me.

Before him I was an innocent, and so ignorant of the ways of the big bad world, and I still remain so happy and grateful that I met him at that time. It's so sad that our relationship ended in the way it did, but I would like to think I learned from my mistakes, and I learned a lot about life from Tom.

I feel I can now look back on my tumultuous life with no regrets whatsoever, and I'm quite adamant that I wouldn't change a thing. I am grateful for the wonderful life I have had so far, and who knows what maybe waits around the corner? I shall welcome every new adventure as always, with curiosity, and as Mickey used to say, "With a little Chablis and snail."

I look at my yesterdays for months past and find them as good a lot of yesterdays as anybody might want. I sit there in the firelight and see them all. The hours that made them were good, and so were the moments that made the hours. I have had responsibilities and work, dangers and pleasure, good friends, and a world without walls to live in.

– Beryl Markham

Acknowledgements

This book could never have been written without the help and support of many people, and first and foremost I am supremely grateful to Fiona Schultz, Managing Director of New Holland Publishers. I owe her an immense debt for her persistence, and her invaluable and detailed help in putting together and making sense of my rambling story.

To my friend and mentor, Mark William Sheehan, who first brought my manuscript to the attention of the New Holland team, thank you for believing in me, and for your inherent faith that we could go somewhere with this memoir. Thank you also for your persistence in keeping my story in front of the people who mattered.

To my dear friend, Shane Boocock, who has been on the side lines all the way, urging me on when I really doubted myself, thank you. And thank you for your tireless re-reading and editing. Without your fulsome (and totally undeserved) praise of my work, I would never have kept going, so a huge thank you to you.

Finally, to all my lovely family and friends, thank you for your ongoing support, and I hope you're not too disappointed in the result!

First published in 2024 by New Holland Publishers
Sydney

Level 1, 178 Fox Valley Road, Wahroonga, NSW 2076, Australia

newhollandpublishers.com

A record of this book is held at the National Library of Australia.

ISBN 9781760796815

Managing Director: Fiona Schultz
Project Editor: Xavier Waterkeyn
Designer: Andrew Davies
Production Director: Arlene Gippert
Printed in China

Keep up with New Holland Publishers:
NewHollandPublishers
@newhollandpublishers